BAPTISTWAY ADULT BIBLE TEACHING GUIDE®

Galatians and
1 & 2 Thessalonians
BUILDING ON A SOLID FOUNDATION

DAVID MAY
MICHAEL WILLIAMS
BRIAN EDWARDS
CHARLES GLIDEWELL
EMILY MARTIN
TYLER PURTLEBAUGH

BAPTISTWAYPRESS®

Dallas, Texas

Galatians and 1 & 2 Thessalonians:
Building On a Solid Foundation—Adult Bible Teaching Guide

BAPTISTWAY PRESS® Management Team
Executive Director, Baptist General Convention of Texas: Randel Everett
Director, Education/Discipleship Center: Chris Liebrum
Director, Bible Study/Discipleship: Phil Miller
Publisher, BAPTISTWAY PRESS®: Ross West

Cover and Interior Design and Production: Desktop Miracles, Inc.
Printing: Data Reproductions Corporation

First edition: September 2009
ISBN–13: 978–1–934731–36–9

How to Make the Best Use of *This* Teaching Guide

Leading a class in studying the Bible is a sacred trust. This *Teaching Guide* has been prepared to help you as you give your best to this important task.

In each lesson, you will find first "Bible Comments" for teachers, to aid you in your study and preparation. The three sections of "Bible Comments" are "Understanding the Context," "Interpreting the Scriptures," and "Focusing on the Meaning." "Understanding the Context" provides a summary overview of the entire background passage that also sets the passage in the context of the Bible book being studied. "Interpreting the Scriptures" provides verse-by-verse comments on the focal passage. "Focusing on the Meaning" offers help with the meaning and application of the focal text.

The second main part of each lesson is "Teaching Plans." You'll find two complete teaching plans in this section. The first is called "Teaching Plan—Varied Learning Activities," and the second is called "Teaching Plan—Lecture and Questions." Choose the plan that best fits your class and your style of teaching. You may also use and adapt ideas from both. Each plan is intended to be practical, helpful, and immediately useful as you prepare to teach.

The major headings in each teaching plan are intended to help you sequence how you teach so as to follow the flow of how people tend to learn. The first major heading, "Connect with Life," provides ideas that will help you begin the class session where your class is and draw your class into the study. The second major heading, "Guide Bible Study," offers suggestions for helping your class engage the Scriptures actively and develop a greater understanding of this portion of the Bible's message. The third major heading, "Encourage Application," is meant to help participants focus on how to respond with their lives to this message.

As you begin the study with your class, be sure to find a way to help your class know the date on which each lesson will be studied. You might use one or more of the following methods:

- In the first session of the study, briefly overview the study by identifying with your class the date on which each lesson will be studied. Lead your class to write the date in the table of contents in their *Study Guides* and on the first page of each lesson.
- Make and post a chart that indicates the date on which each lesson will be studied.
- If all of your class has e-mail, send them an e-mail with the dates the lessons will be studied.
- Provide a bookmark with the lesson dates. You may want to include information about your church and then use the bookmark as an outreach tool, too. A model for a bookmark can be downloaded from www.baptistwaypress.org on the Resources for Adults page.
- Develop a sticker with the lesson dates, and place it on the table of contents or on the back cover.

Here are some steps you can take to help you prepare well to teach each lesson and save time in doing so:

1. Start early in the week before your class meets.

2. If your church's adult Bible study teachers meet for lesson overview and preparation, plan to participate. If your church's adult Bible study teachers don't have this planning time now, look for ways to begin. You, your fellow teachers, and your church will benefit from this mutual encouragement and preparation.

3. Overview the study in the *Study Guide*. Look at the table of contents, and see where this lesson fits in the overall study. Then read or review the study introduction to the book that is being studied.

4. Consider carefully the suggested Main Idea, Question to Explore, and Teaching Aim. These can help you discover the main thrust of this particular lesson.

5. Use your Bible to read and consider prayerfully the Scripture passages for the lesson. Using your Bible in your study and in the class session can provide a positive model to class members to use their own Bibles and give more attention to Bible study themselves. (Each writer of the Bible comments in both the *Teaching Guide* and the

Study Guide has chosen a favorite translation. You're free to use the Bible translation you prefer and compare it with the translations chosen, of course.)

6. After reading all the Scripture passages in your Bible, then read the Bible comments in the *Study Guide*. The Bible comments are intended to be an aid to your study of the Bible. Read also the small articles—"sidebars"—in each lesson. They are intended to provide additional, enrichment information and inspiration and to encourage thought and application. Try to answer for yourself the questions included in each lesson. They're intended to encourage further thought and application, and you can also use them in the class session itself. Continue your Bible study with the aid of the Bible comments included in this *Teaching Guide*.

7. Review the "Teaching Plans" in this *Teaching Guide*. Consider how these suggestions would help you teach this Bible passage in your class to accomplish the teaching aim.

8. Consider prayerfully the needs of your class, and think about how to teach so you can help your class learn best.

9. Develop and follow a lesson plan based on the suggestions in this *Teaching Guide*, with alterations as needed for your class.

10. Enjoy leading your class in discovering the meaning of the Scripture passages and in applying these passages to their lives.

FREE! Additional adult Bible study comments by Dr. Jim Denison (president, The Center for Informed Faith, Dallas, Texas, and theologian-in-residence, Baptist General Convention of Texas) are online at www.baptistwaypress.org and can be downloaded free. These lessons are posted at www.baptistwaypress.org a week in advance of the first Sunday of use.

FREE! Downloadable teaching resource items for use in your class are available at www.baptistwaypress.org! Watch for them in "Teaching Plans" for each lesson. Then go online to www.baptistwaypress.org and click on "Teaching Resource Items" for this study. These items are selected from "Teaching Plans." They are provided online to make lesson preparation easier for hand-outs and similar items. Permission is granted to download these teaching resource items, print them out, copy them as needed, and use them in your class.

ALSO FREE! An additional teaching plan by Dennis Parrott, a veteran Christian education leader, is available each week at www.baptistwaypress.org.

IN ADDITION: Enrichment teaching help is provided in the internet edition of the *Baptist Standard.* Access the *FREE* internet information by checking the *Baptist Standard* website at www.baptiststandard.com. Call 214–630–4571 to begin your subscription to the printed or electronic edition of the *Baptist Standard.*

Writers of This Teaching Guide

Michael E. (Mike) Williams, Sr., wrote "Bible Comments" on Galatians, lessons one through eight. Dr. Williams is dean of the College of Humanities and Social Sciences and professor of history at Dallas Baptist University. He was the founding pastor of Trinity Hills Baptist Church in Fort Worth, Texas, and continues to serve churches as a supply preacher and interim pastor. This is his fourth set of "Bible Comments" to write for BaptistWay.

David May (B.S. Northwest Missouri State University; M.Div., Southern Baptist Theological Seminary; Ph.D., Southern Baptist Theological Seminary) wrote "Bible Comments" on 1 and 2 Thessalonians, lessons nine through thirteen. Dr. May serves as professor of New Testament at Central Baptist Theological Seminary in Shawnee, Kansas. He is also a frequent lecturer and teacher in Baptist congregations in the Midwest. He focuses his writing on articles and essays related to social and cultural contexts of the first-century world. In addition, he is a board member of the Baptist journal *Review & Expositor.*

Charles Glidewell wrote "Teaching Plans" for lessons one through three on Galatians. He is the pastor of Cross Roads Baptist Church in Rotan, Texas. He received the Master of Divinity degree from Logsdon Seminary, Abilene, Texas.

Brian Edwards wrote "Teaching Plans" for lessons four through six on Galatians. He is minister of students at First Baptist Church of Carrollton, Georgia. Before moving to Georgia, he served churches in Texas. He earned the Master of Divinity degree at Logsdon Seminary in Abilene, Texas.

Tyler Purtlebaugh wrote "Teaching Plans" for lessons seven and eight on Galatians. He is a recent graduate of Baptist Theological Seminary at Richmond, Virginia, where he earned the degree of Master of Divinity with a concentration in Christian Education. Tyler and his wife, Renee, live in Louisville, Kentucky.

Emily Martin wrote "Teaching Plans" for lessons nine through thirteen on 1 and 2 Thessalonians. She is a professional writer specializing in business and Christian communication. Emily has written numerous assignments for BAPTISTWAY PRESS®. She and her husband have a son and a daughter and are members of Park Cities Baptist Church, Dallas, Texas.

Galatians and 1 and 2 Thessalonians: Building On a Solid Foundation

DATE OF STUDY

U N I T   O N E

Only By Faith in Christ Jesus

U N I T   T W O

The Gospel in Life

MAIN IDEA
Only the gospel of the grace
of God in Christ is worthy
of our commitment.

QUESTION TO EXPLORE
At what point does
acceptance of differing
viewpoints turn into a denial
of the gospel of Christ?

TEACHING AIM
To lead the class to identify
current substitutes for the
gospel of the grace of God
in Christ and describe
how to respond in light of
Paul's strong statements

LESSON ONE
Only One Gospel

UNIT ONE
**Only By Faith in
Christ Jesus**

BIBLE COMMENTS

Understanding the Context

The area known as Galatia in New Testament times was in central Asia Minor or modern-day Turkey. The Roman province of Galatia stretched from the narrow province of Bithynia that bordered the Black Sea to the province of Pamphylia on the Mediterranean Sea. It was east of the Roman province of Asia where significant New Testament cities like Colossae and Ephesus were located. It was northwest of Tarsus, Paul's hometown. The southern portion of Galatia included the cities of Lystra, Iconium, and Antioch in Pisidia, all of which are mentioned in the New Testament. Paul and Barnabas traveled through this region on their first missionary journey. No direct evidence has been discovered to suggest that Paul ever traveled through the northern part of the province, although some believe he journeyed there on his second missionary trip.

Scholars generally believe that the Galatian peoples originated in central Europe. Some migrated into Britain and became known as Celts. Others migrated to France where they were known as Gauls. Still others eventually migrated to Asia Minor where the indigenous people labeled them Galatians.

Pauline scholars have long debated the dating and audience of Paul's Epistle to the Galatians. Some scholars hold what is called the *North Galatian Theory*. They believe Paul wrote Galatians after the Jerusalem Council in Acts 15 and after his second missionary journey. According to this theory, the recipients of the letter were churches in locations such as Ancyra and Tavium that are not mentioned in the New Testament. Those who hold to an earlier writing of Galatians are proponents of the *South Galatian Theory*. They believe Paul wrote the letter after his first missionary journey and before the Jerusalem Council. Others hold to some sort of hybrid view that combines both approaches.

A segment of Christians known as Judaizers plagued the early churches. Judaizers insisted that Gentile converts must first become Jews, which meant that they must practice circumcision and other ritual practices of Judaism to become Christians. Paul frequently encountered problems throughout Acts with these Jewish Christians. One of the main purposes of the Galatian letter was to deal with the questions raised by these Judaizers.

Interpreting the Scriptures

Greeting (1:1–5)

1:1–2. Paul customarily began his letters by introducing himself. In some of them, he simply introduced himself and others who were with him. In many of his letters, he identified himself by giving his name and then adding that he was "an apostle by the will of God." In Galatians and the Letter to the Romans, Paul found it necessary to qualify even further his apostleship. Here, Paul wrote that Jesus Christ and God the Father chose him for his mission. The highly descriptive introduction offers a clue that Paul intended to deal with difficult issues. He apparently wanted to clarify from the beginning that this message came not just from personal beliefs but from the authority God had given him. He added that this greeting also came from "all the brethren who are with me." Had Paul identified his companions or co-workers, scholars might find it easier to pinpoint more exactly the date of the letter's writing and more precisely who its recipients were. It is possible that Paul may have been identifying those who sympathized with the arguments he would present. In verse 2, Paul simply named the recipients as "the churches of Galatia." This indicates that Paul intended the various churches in that region to circulate his letter.

1:3–5. As was typical in Paul's letters, he opened with a greeting of "grace" and "peace." Paul used this wording with only slight variation in every letter he wrote. In his letters to Timothy, he added an additional word, "mercy." However, Paul did utilize something different in his greeting to the Galatians. Paul always used "grace" in association with Christ. The peace of which Paul wrote is the kind of peace to which he often referred. Most commentators agree that this "peace" parallels the *shalom* of a Hebrew greeting, while Paul applied "grace" as coming solely from Christ. Paul used "grace and peace" to give a blessing to his readers.

Paul's salutations were similar, but not identical. One difference found only in Galatians was Paul's elaboration on the sacrificial death of Jesus. Throughout the New Testament, we find that this self-giving of Jesus resulted in positive consequences. Paul wanted his readers to know that as Christians they were experiencing the Christlike life even while living in an evil age that was, and is, passing away. It is quite possible that Paul introduced this concept at the very beginning of his letter because he planned to hammer home throughout the letter the all-sufficient power of God's grace through Jesus Christ and his sacrifice. It may well be a foreshadowing of Paul's intent to criticize those who sought to add requirements on to God's grace in salvation. He concluded his greeting with a commitment to God's will and with a statement of praise to God.

The Problem in Galatia (1:6–10)

1:6–7. Paul quickly and uncharacteristically jumped immediately to the purpose of his letter. Often, he began his letters with a prayer and some sort of recognition of his recipients' gifts or positive qualities. Even the First Epistle to the Corinthians, one of his most intense letters and critiques of the believers' faith, followed this pattern. In Galatians, however, Paul cut directly to the heart of the matter. The word Paul used that may be translated as "amazed" or *astonished* was a powerful word. Paul could not understand how the Galatians were "deserting" God's message in Christ and how it could happen "so quickly." It is uncertain, though, whether Paul meant that their "deserting" occurred soon after he had been there or soon after these false teachers appeared in Galatia. "Deserting" can also be translated as *departing* or *turning away from*. Paul used the present tense to describe an ongoing process or trend that he hoped to end. Stopping this growing trend in the Galatian churches describes Paul's basic intent for his letter.

Paul vehemently opposed the teaching of the Judaizers (see "Understanding the Context"). As the remainder of the letter will demonstrate, Paul believed their distortion not only caused disruption of the church's work but also muted the believers' experience of grace. Another translation of "distort" is *pervert*. Paul clearly believed these false teachers were confusing the Galatians. In Paul's mind, this false gospel prevented the believers from enjoying the grace that was theirs.

1:8–9. Paul posed a hypothetical case. He went so far as to say that were he or an "angel from heaven" to preach such distortions, it would warrant a curse from God. He used these extreme examples to stress how serious this offense was. Of course, neither he nor an angel would ever do this but, even so, they would be subject to the same judgment as these offenders. One scholar has written that the gospel "is so holy that anyone who independently modifies it brings down the curse of God on his head."[1] Apparently from what Paul wrote in verse 9, he had already warned them about those who would preach a false gospel. This ignored warning may in part explain Paul's strong reaction to their abandonment of the gospel of grace.

1:10. Here Paul began to make the transition to the next section. The Judaizers may have suggested that Paul had preached a watered-down version of the gospel during his visit so he might gain a wider following. They may have insisted they were correcting his error. In other passages, 1 Thessalonians 2:4 for example, Paul clearly stated that he sought not to please people but to please God, whereas the Judaizers may have claimed that Paul was seeking to please people. Paul wrote that he was a "bond-servant" or *slave* of Christ. In the passage that we will discuss in the next lesson, Paul proceeded to defend his apostleship.

Focusing on the Meaning

There are those who might accuse Paul of narrow-mindedness. Like Paul, the Judaizers believed that one was saved through Jesus Christ. They undoubtedly believed that Jesus was Savior. As long as they trusted Christ, then shouldn't they have been welcomed as fellow followers? Was Paul too harsh on them and their teaching?

Paul clearly considered God's grace so powerful and great that he believed any attempt to add requirements to it for salvation muted its significance. Paul may have feared that any sort of additional requirements to salvation would ultimately result in some sort of works righteousness. Paul taught that God's grace alone was sufficient. Jesus had paid the price to purchase humanity's redemption. Nothing should be added to that. To do so endangers the very truth of the gospel.

Paul was saying that salvation was God's gift, whereas the gospel proclaimed by the Judaizers was a different gospel entirely. As we shall see, they were insisting on additional requirements. They were making God's gift into a form of a purchase. God's grace is a complete and total gift. It cannot be earned, but it must be accepted. When we accept that gift and recognize the fullness of it, we honor our gracious, gift-giving Lord. When we share that gift with others, we become further participants in God's great grace. As Paul wrote in 2 Corinthians 9:15, "Thanks be to God for his indescribable gift!"

TEACHING PLANS

Teaching Plan—Varied Learning Activities

Connect with Life

1. Think of one or more heroic *rescue* scenarios (fire rescue, life guard, being tied to train tracks, etc.). Have willing participants act these rescue scenarios out. Consider taking the initiative and volunteering yourself. Have fun and ham it up a bit. This activity will serve not only as a good object lesson but also as a helpful ice breaker. After the fun is over, discuss what occurred during the rescue(s). Affirm that we as Christians have been rescued from death and eternal separation from God by the selfless action of God through Christ. This is the gospel.

2. Next, refer to the rescue scenarios, and say something to the effect that the facts behind a story are usually very important. Begin a discussion about the possible frustration and even anger that might occur after hearing someone get the facts of a very important story wrong (for example, identifying another person as the hero in one of the above rescue scenarios). Ask the class whether anyone has ever experienced the frustration of someone getting the facts of a story wrong. Inform the class that this analogy can begin to help

us identify with the frustration and even anger the Apostle Paul felt toward those who were giving a false testimony about the gospel.

Guide Bible Study

3. Have volunteers read Galatians 1:1–10 in two or three translations represented in the class. Ask the class to listen for some of the key points made in the passage. Tape a large piece of paper to the wall and have a marker on hand. Lead the group to list the powerful words Paul used in Galatians 1:1–10 that seem to indicate his passion about the situation at the church in Galatia (for example, from the NIV, "astonished," "deserting," "confusion," "pervert," "condemned"). Ask, *Why do you think Paul was so disturbed by what is going on in this church?*

4. Explain Paul's use of the word "different" using the information in the *Study Guide*.

5. Divide the class into two or more groups (no more than six people each). Have each group suggest at least three substitutes for the gospel of God in Christ that are held by many in our culture. Then have each group suggest three appropriate responses to these false teachings. Have the groups come together and share their findings. Next, refer to the *Study Guide* comments about being narrow-minded under the heading "Paul's Concern (1:6–10)." Explore together possible responses to the view that Paul's position about the gospel was too narrow-minded.

6. Have a debate between two groups. Have one side argue the following: *Since I am saved by grace, I can live however I want.* Have the other side argue: *Even though I am saved by grace, I must still follow God's teachings.* Discuss the proper place of works in our relationship with God.

Encourage Application

7. Lead the class to consider things they might put into a note to God thanking him especially for rescuing them from this "present evil age." Invite suggestions after a few moments. Lead participants to

write a short note to God thanking him for his grace in Christ. Encourage the class to keep this note with them throughout the week to serve as a reminder of God's selfless action on our behalf.

8. Close with prayer. Offer both thanksgiving and petition—thanksgiving for God's wonderful mercy and grace, and specific petition for those who may be being led astray by another gospel that is really no gospel at all.

Teaching Plan—Lecture and Questions

Connect with Life

1. Before class, write the two Greek words for *another* on a board at the front of the class (*allos* and *heteron*). Begin the class by summarizing the two paragraphs that begin the lesson in the *Study Guide*. Then refer to the two Greek words. Use the information about these words under "Paul's Concern (1:6–10)" in the *Study Guide* to explain that while both of these words are translated the same way in English, they have different meanings. Use two different kinds of fruit for an object lesson as the writer does in the *Study Guide*. Explain to the class that a group of teachers known as the Judaizers had presented another gospel of a different kind to the church in Galatia.

Guide Bible Study

2. Enlist someone to read Galatians 1:1–10 while the class listens for the problem with which Paul was dealing in these verses. After the reading, call attention to verses 1 and 2. Ask the class what difference they think it makes that Paul was "sent not from men nor by man, but by Jesus Christ and God the Father." After allowing a short time of discussion, display a poster on the wall that says, "Wanted: Paul." Underneath this heading, write, "Charges." Then number 1–3 and write a charge beside each number (1. not an apostle, 2. no gospel at all, 3. loose living). Explain these charges against

Paul using the information under the section "Paul's Calling" in the *Study Guide.*

3. Next, write the words "The Rescuer" on the left side of the board. Invite the class to share fitting characteristics of one who rescues others. List responses on the board. Then start another column and write the words "The Rescued." Ask the class to share fitting characteristics of one who is rescued by someone else (needs help, unable to rescue himself or herself). After this exercise bring attention to Paul's words in verses 3–4.

4. Share some thoughts about what God through Christ has rescued you from (the parts of this present evil age from which you have struggled to be free). Encourage others to share their experience of being rescued.

5. Point the class to the small article in the *Study Guide* titled "A Question," and lead them to respond to the question. Say, *One might argue that this young ruler was guilty of trying to receive a righteousness through works.* Then ask, *What are some other substitutes for the gospel of grace that are floating around in our culture?* After this discussion, refer to and summarize the last two paragraphs under the section titled "Paul's Concern" in the *Study Guide,* on narrow-mindedness and tolerance.

Encourage Application

6. Lead the class to contemplate the beauty of the wonderful gospel of God. Have the class close their eyes as you read one of the accounts of Jesus' crucifixion (perhaps Luke 23:33–46). Remind the class that we had nothing to do with God's plan of the cross. God came to us, and in Christ we have indeed been rescued.

7. Close with a time of prayer, thanking God for his gospel.

NOTES

1. Herman N. Ridderbos, *The Epistle of Paul to the Churches of Galatia* (Grand Rapids, MI: Wm. B. Eerdmans Publishing Co., 1953, 1981 reprint), 50–51.

FOCAL TEXT
Galatians 1:11–24

BACKGROUND
Galatians 1:11–24

MAIN IDEA
Paul's experience with Christ led him to view life through the lens of the gospel rather than human tradition and live with boldness in response to God's gracious call.

QUESTION TO EXPLORE
In what ways do we need to learn to view life through the lens of the gospel rather than human tradition and live with boldness in response to God's gracious call?

TEACHING AIM
To lead the class to decide on areas in which they need to learn to view life through the lens of the gospel rather than human tradition and live with boldness in response to God's call

LESSON TWO
The Difference the Gospel Makes

UNIT ONE
Only By Faith in Christ Jesus

BIBLE COMMENTS

Understanding the Context

One of the keys to understanding Paul's writing is to recognize that he did not expect his readers to believe what he said based on only his personal authority. Paul always stressed that his authority came from Christ's call to be an apostle of the gospel. It did not come from other people or from his personal experience, although certainly his experience expressed and illustrated the gospel and the God Paul proclaimed. Paul's experience of God's grace originated in the generosity of God, and not through any effort by Paul. Paul simply accepted the gift. He expressed his testimony in this passage to defend his ministry and to demonstrate from whom his authority came. His story equipped him with a holy boldness since he knew his power came from God.

Interpreting the Scriptures

Paul's Defense (1:11–12)

1:11. Paul had ended the previous paragraph (Galatians 1:6–10) by protesting that he had not sought the favor of people. In verse 11, he further elaborated and began a defense of his apostleship. He wanted his readers to understand clearly that he did not rely on the authority of human beings but on God's authority alone. The phrase, "I would have you know," can also be translated as something like *I want you to be clear.* A Baptist scholar of an earlier generation, A.T. Robertson, indicated the next statement is a play on words in the original language, literally reading, *the gospel that I gospelized to you.*[1] The phrase that follows, "not according to man," can mean that the gospel Paul preached was *not made up by man.* If human beings did not create it, then by implication it must have come from God. Note that despite the harsh words Paul used in the preceding passage, he still addressed the Galatians as "brethren" ("brothers and sisters," NRSV).

1:12. Paul stressed that the revelation he received came not from human beings and neither was it taught him by human beings. He insisted that his experience came not from memorization and drill as he had likely experienced in the rabbinic schools of Judaism. The revelation he called to their attention came directly from Jesus Christ. He referred to this as a reminder of his Damascus road experience and the intense relationship Paul formed with Jesus Christ.

Paul's Testimony of His Early Life and Call (1:13–17)

1:13–14. Paul began his testimony by reminding the Galatians that they had heard about his upbringing in traditional Jewish beliefs. The word he used, "manner," can easily be translated as *behavior* or *conduct*. He described this conduct in the Jewish religion in such a way as to indicate that it was his complete way of life. He utilized a twofold example. First, he indicated that he intensely persecuted Christians. His persecution was so intense that he tried to destroy the church. His testimony here verifies what Acts records. Furthermore, he stated that he was so zealous that his Judaism exceeded that of his peers. The language he utilized clearly demonstrated that Paul's Jewish credentials were impeccable. Simply put, Paul's testimony indicated he fanatically followed the strictest observances of Judaism. No one could have been more religious in Judaism than Paul. Because of his learning and commitment, Paul would have reached the highest Jewish circles had he remained in the Jewish faith.

Clearly, however, Paul implied that this behavior was inadequate. In Philippians 3:4–8, Paul gave a more complete description of the merits he accumulated in his Jewish faith. But in Philippians 3:8, he said all he had lost was "rubbish."

1:15. Paul contrasted his negative prior experience in legalistic tradition against the positives of his ministry in the gospel. He stated that God's good pleasure was to set him apart from birth and to call him to a special ministry. "Set apart" may be translated as *ordained,* and Paul used a construct that was similar to that of the Old Testament prophets. For example, the language Paul invoked is similar to that given in the call of Jeremiah (Jeremiah 1:5–6). Paul's experience of God's grace in the gospel trumped the Jewish religious background that had once been so important to him.

1:16–17. Paul used the phrase "His Son" or "God's Son" fifteen times in his letters. In his later letters, he used a different phrase, denoting Jesus as "Christ Jesus" or as "Lord." Perhaps Paul used this phrasing here to identify better the connection of Jesus with *Yahweh*, since he had been emphasizing his Jewish heritage. Nevertheless, Paul's identification with the One he formerly persecuted became so strong that he understood his call was to preach among the nations—that is, to preach to the non-Jewish peoples. The revelation became so strong he did not go immediately to Jerusalem to consult with the apostles there but instead went into Arabia. He did not specify exactly where he went in Arabia, and neither did he indicate his purpose there, although some suggest he may have engaged in mission work. Others suggest he sought solitude and may have utilized the time for reflection and to await a call from God regarding his future mission. After that he returned to Damascus. Paul did not say why but he may have wanted to affirm the support of the church in Damascus and continue his training and ministry before he went to Jerusalem.

Paul's First Trip to Jerusalem (1:18–24)

1:18–19. Paul told the Galatians that after "three years" he went to Jerusalem. This probably means three years after his conversion and was probably his first visit since he left Jerusalem on his trip of persecution. Apparently Paul sought to establish contact with the apostles. He specifically mentioned Cephas, typically understood as Peter, and James the brother of Jesus. He visited with Peter for a little more than two weeks. As can be determined from reading Acts, both Peter and Paul held significant positions in the early church. However, the language used in this passage in no way suggests Paul had a lesser position, that he sought the approval of the other apostles, or that he believed such approval was necessary to validate his ministry.

1:20–21. In verse 20, Paul stressed that he told the truth in recounting his time in Jerusalem. Such affirmations are found frequently throughout Paul's writing. He mentioned further that he spent time in Syria and

Cilicia. He preached and evangelized. Some suggest that some of the persecution he mentioned in 2 Corinthians 11:23–29 occurred on these journeys. We need to remember that Acts does not record every aspect of Paul's life and ministry.

1:22–24. While the churches at Jerusalem and Damascus would have known Paul by sight, the churches in Judea would not have recognized him. Paul testified that even though they had not seen him, they had heard about his powerful testimony. Their response validated Paul's ministry.

Focusing on the Meaning

Human tradition and the personal experience of Judaism bound Paul for all his early life. If earning God's favor could have been accomplished by obedience to tradition and personal merit, then Paul would have earned all the points possible. Yet, when he encountered Jesus on the Damascus road, his life radically changed. No longer did tradition bind him. He became, as one New Testament scholar has entitled a book about Paul, "Apostle of the Heart Set Free."[2]

The human tendency for people to believe that they can earn or merit God's favor solely by their behaviors persists. Nothing could be further from the truth. While certainly we can hope our behavior will represent our faith well, our works do not earn salvation. Only the acceptance of God's grace can give us the relationship with God that we require and desire.

Paul lived a life of holy boldness after he experienced God's grace. He relinquished all he had done and tried to do, and he accepted the assignment of preaching the gospel he had received. This happened only as Paul saw life through the gospel.

For the first twenty-nine years of my life, I had perfect vision. In fact, during my high school baseball days, eye tests showed that I actually had 20–15 vision. I could see at twenty feet what most people could see only at fifteen.

However, about the time I turned thirty, my wife and I were on a trip to New Orleans. I kept missing turns because I couldn't read road signs. She determined, and I finally conceded, that I needed glasses. I had become near-sighted. Sure enough, after we returned I went to the eye doctor and got my first pair of glasses. I began to see and notice things I had been missing. I could see individual leaves on trees. In the church softball league, the fly balls were much easier to judge than they had been before. My wife no longer had to read road signs for me. She felt safe riding with me again! The new *lens* that my eyes had received gave my vision fresh perspective.

In the same way, we too can experience a new perspective on life when we begin to view life through the lens of God's grace. We can receive a holy boldness to be on mission for God when we truly recognize that what we have done in ourselves is inadequate and then celebrate the grace God has given us. Like Paul, we can see life through the lens of the gospel and bring greater glory to God by our lives.

TEACHING PLANS

Teaching Plan—Varied Learning Activities

Connect with Life

1. Begin by referring to and quoting the first part of the Main Idea in the *Study Guide*. State: *Paul's experience with Christ led him to view life through the lens of the gospel rather than human tradition.* Divide the class into two groups and have them move to opposite sides of the room. One side will be the *lens of human tradition* and the other side will be the *lens of the gospel.* Have one side begin by saying a word or a phrase that they believe in, and have the other side counter with a word or phrase of their own as soon as possible. (For example, the human tradition side might say, *The law must be upheld at all costs* or *Keeping the rules is what's important.* The gospel side might counter with the sentence, *Christ's love has overcome the law.*)

2. Now state the second half of the Main Idea. Say, *live with boldness in response to God's gracious call.* Now guide the class to people—perhaps in their lives—who have lived with boldness in response to God's gracious call. Allow time for class members to share these inspiring stories.

Guide Bible Study

3. Enlist someone to read Galatians 1:11–16a. Ask the class to listen for how Paul described himself, noting the differences between his character before and after he received the gospel. After the Scripture reading, receive reports about how Paul described himself. Write responses on the board (such as these: he received the gospel through a revelation of Jesus Christ; he was a violent persecutor of the church).

4. Create a poster as a visual aid. Number 1–4 . Write on the poster (or board) the four elements of God's call as described in the *Study Guide* under the heading "Before God's Call (1:13–16a)." Refer to each element, and ask the class to call out words that come to mind when reading each one. (For example, the statement, "the call comes from God," may bring the word *grace* to someone's mind. Another person may think of the sentence, *God is in charge.*)

5. Invite someone to read Galatians 1:16b–20 while the group listens for what Paul did after God called him. Point out that Paul's call was from God and not from human commissioning. Lead the class to trace what Paul did. Along the way, state that the *Study Guide* (see paragraph 2 under "After God's Call") indicates that after receiving his calling from the risen Lord on the Damascus road, Paul went to the Arabian desert and did these things: communed with God; contemplated the miraculous change in his life and what it meant; and studied again the promises of the Old Testament that are fulfilled in Christ. All of these helped to prepare Paul's heart for the work God had called him to do. Divide the class into two groups. Ask one group to write down some advantages that come with preparing for any given task. Ask the other group to write down some drawbacks that can come with failing to give adequate time to preparation. Have each group

share their thoughts and discuss the importance of preparing for what God has called us to do.

6. Read Galatians 1:21–24. State: *Surely Paul was uncertain about some things. He was after all embarking on a ministry that went against everything he had always believed. Also, it seemed that Paul had a lot of enemies who were constantly trying to twist his message into something else. We are not the first and will not be the last to experience a bold call to action from God. Serving God often involves a lot of uncertainty. However, we can always be certain that God will both empower and equip us for the work that he has called us to do.* Invite someone to summarize the small article, "Roger Williams," in the *Study Guide.*

Encourage Application

7. Lead the class to suggest the differences that occurred in Paul's life when he began to view life through the lens of the gospel rather than of human tradition. Ask the class to name areas in which they think we need to do the same.

8. Assign various individuals in the group to read the following passages: Romans 12:6–8; 1 Corinthians 12:4–11; Ephesians 4:11–12. Encourage the group to listen for the gifts mentioned in these passages and to consider their own gifts. Refer to the small article "To Apply This Lesson to Your Life" in the *Study Guide.* Lead the group to consider what might happen in their lives if they actually did this.

9. Refer to Galatians 1:24. State: *While it is important that we recognize the ways in which God has blessed and gifted us, we should also take the initiative to be aware of one another's gifts.* Now take the remainder of the class time for this exercise of encouragement. Single out one person in the class and allow every other person in the class to complete this statement about that one person: "I glorify God because of you because. . . ." Allow each person to be singled out and encouraged, including yourself as the teacher.

10. End with a prayer of thanksgiving for one another and for God's grace in our lives.

Teaching Plans—Lecture and Questions

Connect with Life

1. Write the word "Boldness" on a chalkboard or whiteboard. Ask the class to call out what comes to mind when thinking about this word. Next, ask the class to share stories about people acting with boldness for God. Finally, have a volunteer read the Main Idea from the *Study Guide*.

Guide Bible Study

2. Enlist someone to read Galatians 1:11–12 while the class listens for the source of the gospel Paul preached. Point out statements in the *Study Guide* under the heading "The Source of the Gospel (1:11–12)" about the authenticity of the Christian faith. Ask, *How do we know from Paul's experience that the gospel of Jesus Christ is from God?* Emphasize: (1) Only God can bring about such a radical change in someone's life as occurred with Paul. (2) The *proof* for Christianity is found in the arena of human life. (3) When Christianity is tried, it works.

3. Give a brief lecture on the paradigm of calling as it is discussed in the *Study Guide* under the heading "Before God's Call (1:13–16a)." Point out that the four parts of the paradigm of Paul's calling are: (1) the call came from God; (2) the call was rooted in God's grace; (3) the call had been issued at Paul's birth; (4) the calling was focused in a particular area. It may be helpful to compare these aspects of calling to God's calling of people in the Old Testament (such as Moses in Exodus 3:1—4:17; Isaiah in Isaiah 6; Jeremiah in Jeremiah 1:1–10).

4. Invite someone to read Galatians 1:16b–24 while the class listens for the places to which Paul went. If a map of Paul's missionary journeys is available, draw attention to the places mentioned in Galatians 1:16b–21 (Arabia, Damascus, Jerusalem, Syria, Cilicia). Refer to the first sentence under the heading "After God's Call (1:16b–20)" in the *Study Guide*. Point out that this is the reason

Paul described his travels: "To reaffirm the divine source of his call, Paul reviewed his activities immediately after his conversion." Next, refer to 1:20 and then to the question asked in the *Study Guide* in the final paragraph of this same section: "Why was Paul so anxious for the Galatian Christians to hear the truth?" Suggest these answers:

- A group known as the Judaizers was spreading false rumors about Paul.
- One rumor stated that when Paul went to Jerusalem he really went there to get input from people in the Jerusalem church.
- Paul was also accused of twisting the truth of God for his own personal gain.

Encourage Application

5. Refer to verse 24. Point out that the Judean churches were "glorifying God because of" Paul in contrast to the conflict occurring in the Galatian churches. Ask, *Why do you think the Judean churches were doing that?* Refer to verse 23. Point out that Paul was now seeing life through the lens of the gospel rather than that of human tradition and was not living with boldness in response to God's gracious call. Ask, *In what ways do you think we need to do that ourselves?* Receive reports.

6. Lead the class to answer questions 1, 2, and 5 in the *Study Guide*.

7. Guide class members to reflect on questions 3 and 4 privately. Encourage class members to pray as they reflect on these two questions.

NOTES

1. A. T. Robertson, "Galatians," *Word Pictures in the New Testament*, vol. IV (Nashville: Broadman Press, 1931), 277–278.

2. F. F. Bruce, *Paul, Apostle of the Heart Set Free* (Grand Rapids, MI: William B. Eerdmans Publishing, 1977, 1986).

FOCAL TEXT
Galatians 2:1–10

BACKGROUND
Galatians 2:1–10

MAIN IDEA
When our identity as Christians is defined by the gospel and not by culture, we find common ground for living and serving in unity.

QUESTION TO EXPLORE
What would it take for all of us to get along?

TEACHING AIM
To lead adults to identify elements in the encounter of Paul, Barnabas, and Titus with the Jerusalem leaders that would bring the group and your church closer together

LESSON THREE

United By the Gospel

UNIT ONE
Only By Faith in Christ Jesus

BIBLE COMMENTS

Understanding the Context

The gospel of Jesus Christ exists in various tensions. One tension is between living in the faith and living in a world that does not always understand the beliefs and practices of those who identify themselves as Christians. Only after people encounter the transforming power of God through Jesus Christ is it possible to understand the differences that occur between the lives of Christians and non-Christians.

A second tension occurs between different groups within the Christian faith. Splits, divisions, disagreements, and downright fighting litter the pages of church history. One only needs to look in virtually every American town or city to see the results of these divisions. Christianity split between Roman Catholic Church and Eastern Orthodox Church in 1054 in an event known as "The Great Schism." In Western civilization, the Protestant Reformation, which began in 1517, led to the fragmentation of the Western church. The succeeding centuries have only further complicated the situation.

While Christianity has faced many challenges to its existence from outside persecution throughout the centuries, possibly the greatest threat to Christianity has come from within the church itself. Sometimes the finer points of Christian doctrine lead to debate and division. This doctrinal debate is sometimes necessary to maintain the integrity of the gospel. At other times, churches divide over issues that seem ridiculous to outsiders. Paul considered the controversy over the gospel a critical concern. He believed it affected the very essence of the gospel, his mission, and the future path of Christianity. In essence, would Gentiles have to become Jewish before they could become Christian?

Interpreting the Scriptures

The Power of Revelation (2:1–3)

2:1. Scholars are uncertain about where the "fourteen years" fit into Paul's life. Paul may have meant either fourteen years after his conversion or fourteen years after his first visit to Jerusalem. It is uncertain exactly which visit Paul referred to at this point. Was it the one in Acts 11:30 or the Jerusalem Council visit (Acts 15)? Nevertheless, he did tell his readers that Barnabas, another Jewish Christian, and Titus, a Gentile Christian, went with him. The appearance of Titus may suggest that it was the latter visit rather than the former.

2:2. Paul indicated that the reason for his visit was a revelation he received. He did not state how he received it or exactly what the revelation was except that he went to Jerusalem because of it.

When Paul appeared before the leaders in Jerusalem, he reported that he "submitted" or *laid out* for them what he had been teaching and preaching about the gospel. Paul was not wavering about what he preached. Rather, it was quite possible that he submitted his teaching to the brethren in Jerusalem either because of the criticism he had received or perhaps because it concerned the whole Christian community. Paul probably realized that it was important that individual missionaries not go off and preach whatever they chose. That Paul chose to submit his teaching to the church leaders demonstrated how important he believed this decision to be. So even though Paul had received a powerful and compelling revelation, he wanted to share it privately with the leadership in Jerusalem. Paul's implication in the latter part of this verse was that his beliefs had not changed. He did not tailor his gospel to different situations that arose.

2:3. This verse and those that follow are difficult to interpret. In a different situation, Paul required Timothy to be circumcised, but he made it clear in this verse that Titus was not circumcised. The difference was that Timothy was half-Jewish because he had a Jewish mother. It is possible that Paul had Timothy circumcised so that Timothy could be effective in ministering to either Jews or Gentiles. Since Titus was a Gentile, Paul did not require him to conform to Jewish custom. Paul believed this action was consistent with the revelation he had received.

The Importance of Relationship (2:4–5)

2:4. The Jews believed that circumcision represented their covenant with God. Apparently, some of the Jewish-Christians could not imagine a new covenant with God that did not include circumcision. Thus, some Jewish Christians insisted that circumcision be part of the Christian faith. On the other hand, the Christian church is built around relationships rather than ritual observances. One relationship is the personal one that the individual has with God. Another relationship is that which the believers have with one another through the church. Paul indicated in this verse that the concept of relationship had been violated. He stated that the criticism of Titus being uncircumcised occurred because of those "false brethren secretly brought in." In the original language, "false" is the root of our word *pseudo*. Paul used this strong word to indicate the depth of violation that had occurred. Paul further elaborated by writing that these false brethren "sneaked in to spy out." The adjective was commonly utilized to describe "spies and traitors who infiltrate an opposing camp."[1] Paul classified these infiltrators thusly to link them to the "agitators in Galatia who were trying to impose" Hebrew law and customs on Gentile Christians. This type of language insinuated an ominous intent. Paul's last phrase in this verse stated his concern that the liberty Christians experienced in Christ might be replaced with "bondage."

2:5. Paul insisted, however, that despite the infiltration and the havoc that these Judaizing Christians might have wrought, he remained faithful to his mission and to the pledge he had made to the gospel. He specifically stated that he was completely unyielding so he might be loyal to the truth. By remaining loyal to the truth, Paul was not only remaining faithful to the gospel but also to the relationship he had with the Galatian Christians.

The Need for Relevance (2:6–10)

2:6. Paul declared that the pillars in the early church, James, John, and Cephas (Peter), accepted the grace he received and the message he shared. But before he wrote this, he insisted that all people are equal in God's sight. Paul was most definitely not star struck.

2:7–8. In these verses, Paul clarified that his call was to the Gentiles ("the uncircumcised"). Paul insisted that his mission be considered as equivalent to that of Peter to the Jews. His use of the word "entrusted" is critical here. Paul commonly used this word to describe his actions.

He insisted that the same Lord who effectively worked in Peter and his mission also worked in Paul and his mission. God gave each of them similar authority.

2:9. Verse 9 picks up where verse 7 left off. The "pillars" of the New Testament church accepted the grace and the mission God had given Paul and Barnabas. The "right hand of fellowship" suggested that all were equal in the spreading of the gospel and that such an extension validated what Paul and Barnabas did and were doing among the Gentiles. It also suggested that they were unified in their relationship. Such a unity acknowledged the need that the gospel be relevant in all racial, cultural, and national settings.

2:10. The only qualifier the apostles placed on Paul and Barnabas was that they remember the poor in their extension of the gospel. Paul exclaimed that he certainly complied with this admonition. Like the extension of fellowship in the preceding verse, this common mission suggested the unity that existed between Paul and Barnabas and the church at Jerusalem.

Focusing on the Meaning

When the Great Depression began in 1929 with the crash of the stock market, a massive economic crisis hit the United States. Efforts by President Herbert Hoover and the United States Congress were unsuccessful in alleviating the crisis. Unemployment soared to almost twenty-five percent by 1933, and millions of other Americans found themselves under-employed. Banks foreclosed on farms and homes, and more than 5,000 banks closed. Millions of Americans had their life savings wiped out.

In 1932, American voters elected Franklin D. Roosevelt in a landslide backlash against Hoover. After Roosevelt's inauguration in March of 1933, he and the Congress energetically attacked the crisis with an *alphabet soup* of legislation. Acronyms like FDIC (Federal Deposit Insurance Corporation), SEC (Securities and Exchange Commission), and CCC (Civilian Conservation Corps) became indicative of Roosevelt's efforts to restore the nation's prosperity. Over time, this program known as the

New Deal also became recognized as the *three Rs—relief, reform,* and *recovery.* While the New Deal and these programs did not totally end the Great Depression, they did stabilize the economy and make life better for many struggling Americans.[2]

This passage of Scripture demonstrates the necessity of *three Rs* in transmitting the gospel—*revelation, relationship,* and *relevance.* These remain critical today in conveying the message of the gospel. Through the miracle of inspired Scripture, Christians have God's *revelation.* The Holy Spirit enlightens believers as we share God's revelation in worship, witness, and teaching. Tremendous power exists through God's revelation. It also remains important for believers to build and strengthen *relationships* in conveying this revelation and maintaining and extending the ministry of the church. At the same time, we must continually search for ways to make revelation *relevant* to the world in which we live without surrendering to culture. A dynamic tension must remain between revelation and reason. Likewise, churches and believers must build relationships without jettisoning structure and be relevant in today's world without becoming captive to the culture in which we live.

TEACHING PLANS

Teaching Plan—Varied Learning Activities

Connect with Life

1. Begin this session with a friendly competition. Have some cups (plastic, paper) available. Divide the class into two teams. Tell the class the goal is to see which team can build a pyramid out of the cups the fastest. The first team to get their pyramid built, using all of their cups, wins. Here's the catch. On each team there will be a designated *windbag.* His or her job is to blow the other team's pyramid down at will. The windbag on each team may not be restrained in any way but must be allowed to blow the other team's pyramid down at will at a time of his or her choosing. After allowing the

teams several minutes for this activity, move into the next part of
the lesson by drawing attention to the obvious fact that the activity
would have been much easier without the *windbags* in the game.
Say, *It is surprising how even in trying to accomplish the work of
the church, people seem—intentionally?—to get in each other's way
sometimes. In Galatians 2:1–10 Paul remembered how he and other
church members worked together to accomplish God's work.*

Guide Bible Study

2. Summarize briefly the previous study on Galatians 1:11–24. Enlist
   someone to read Galatians 2:1–2 while the class listens for the
   events described in the verses. Next, have the class turn to the Book
   of Acts and allow each member to read Acts 15:1–29 silently. Third,
   assign the parts of *Narrator, a Judaizer* (for the quotes in Acts 15:1,
   5), *Peter,* and *James.* Now have these people read Acts 15:1–29 as
   the rest of the class follows. Explain that the first-century church
   struggled with the question of what a person had to do in order to
   become a Christian. Affirm what the *Study Guide* says at the end
   of the first paragraph under the heading "Paul's Trip to Jerusalem
   (2:1–6)": "Both the Jerusalem council [in Acts 15] and Paul in his
   Galatian letter support the conclusion that salvation comes by faith
   alone."

3. Divide the class into two groups. One group represents the "pillars" of the church and Paul, while the other group represents the
   Judaizers, or those who believed that a person had to observe the
   Jewish law in order to become a Christian. Instruct each group
   to review Galatians 2:1–10 and suggest ideas that describe their
   group. For example, for Paul's group one might write the words
   "grace," "mercy," or "freedom," while the words "works," "ritual,"
   or "burden" might be used to describe the Judaizers. Write suggestions in two columns on a markerboard or poster. Allow each group
   to explain the words they chose. After comparing, see whether the
   groups can think of new words or phrases to describe each other.

4. Invite someone to read Galatians 2:7–10 while the class listens for
   ideas about how the church leaders responded to Paul. Write these
   three words on a markerboard or poster: "Salvation"; "Fellowship";

"Evangelism." Note that the *Study Guide* indicates under the heading "The Outcome of Paul's Trip (2:7–10)" that these were the three important issues at stake in the meeting. Refer to this portion of the *Study Guide,* and either summarize or invite participants to summarize each issue. Refer to and summarize the one condition Paul set forth. On "Evangelism" and the one condition—remembering the poor—share what your church is doing in each area. Lead the class to respond to the following question for each area: *What kind of grade would Jesus give our church in relationship to this area? Why do you think our church would receive this grade?*

5. Tape a large piece of paper to the wall. For the title, write the following sentence from the *Study Guide*: "Collaboration and not competition is the key." Next, post this information:

   (1) Spiritual gifts

   (2) Forms of worship

   (3) Size of church

   Point out that the *Study Guide* suggests that the church needs to learn to appreciate diversity within the family of God in order to be successful. Take each one of these items and have the class list how each item may have different expressions (differing spiritual gifts, forms of worship, church sizes). After compiling your list, guide the class to think of the benefits that come with each kind of item.

Encourage Application

6. Lead the group to identify elements in the encounter of Paul, Barnabas, and Titus with the Jerusalem leaders that would bring the group and your church closer together. Emphasize the importance of the good news of God's grace. Encourage each person to write a brief answer to this study's Question to Explore, "What would it take for all of us to get along?" Give class members time to contemplate and write their answers down. Allow those who are willing to share their answers out loud.

7. Read John 17:18–23. Conclude with a prayer for the unity of the group and of God's church.

Teaching Plan—Lecture and Questions

Connect with Life

1. Bring a tightly-sealed jar to class with oil and water in it. At the beginning of class shake the jar so that the two mix together. While the oil and water separate, explain that this is a good way of thinking about how Jews and Gentiles mixed in the ancient world. (They didn't.) Another idea for beginning the session is to tell the illustration about working together from the introductory paragraphs to this lesson in the *Study Guide.*

Guide Bible Study

2. Enlist someone to read Galatians 2:1–6. Begin by noting the three questions the *Study Guide* mentions under the heading "Paul's Trip to Jerusalem (2:1–6)." Use information from the *Study Guide* to explain the answers to these three questions. Here is a brief outline:

   (1) Which trip to Jerusalem was Paul referring to in Galatians 2:1? Paul's trip to Jerusalem is probably the one recorded in Acts 15, although opinions vary on this.

   (2) What did Paul do for fourteen years? Paul preached in Tarsus, labored with Barnabas in Antioch, went on a relief mission to Jerusalem, and then went on his first missionary journey.

   (3) Why did Paul go to Jerusalem after these fourteen years? Paul went to Jerusalem in response to a revelation from God. Since a group known as the Judaizers was contradicting Paul's message of grace, Paul went to Jerusalem to present his case to the church there.

3. Help the class understand the various groups involved in this lesson's Scripture passage. Refer to the small article "Gentiles" in the *Study Guide.* Summarize briefly who Gentiles were. Then draw a clear distinction between Paul and the "pillars" of the church in Jerusalem and the group known as the Judaizers. Point out that

the Judaizers maintained that a Gentile had to become a practicing Jew (receive circumcision, observe the food laws, etc.) before becoming a Christian. Paul and his friends rejected this notion and taught that salvation was simply received by having faith in the risen Lord.

4. Read Galatians 2:7–10 while the group listens for how the church leaders at Jerusalem responded to Paul. (Add insights from Acts 15 if this seems helpful and if there is time.) Using the information in the *Study Guide* under the heading "The Outcome of Paul's Trip (2:7–10)," give a brief lecture on the three issues at stake: salvation; fellowship; and evangelism. Continue by explaining the condition Paul put on the agreement ("remember the poor").

5. Explore the following questions with the class:

    (1) Do you know of a project that failed because people did not cooperate?

    (2) What is the best example you have seen of an accomplishment coming to pass because of the teamwork of a group?

    (3) What are some good lessons you have learned about working well with others?

    (4) Who taught you these lessons?

6. Read Galatians 2:10 again. As a class, explore the following case studies:

    (1) When talking to a person in your church, the subject of poverty comes up. After talking for several minutes you get the feeling that this person has a negative view of poor people. He makes comments such as these: *As a general rule, poor people are lazy. God helps those who help themselves. We were poor growing up, and we didn't take handouts from anyone.* Based on the teachings in the gospels and the letters of Paul, such as Galatians, how do you respond to this kind of attitude?

    (2) A person calls you and asks whether you can help out by buying some groceries for him and his family. You are delighted to help. A couple of weeks later you receive

the same call from the same person. Again, you provide assistance. Two months later you are still regularly getting calls from this same man wanting help with everything from groceries to gasoline to medical expenses. How should Christians handle these kinds of situations?

(3) A foreign exchange student was staying with an American family for the spring semester. On Sunday the family took their guest to church and introduced him to the pastor and staff and the rest of the congregation. While the pastor and host family were giving the exchange student a tour of the church, they entered into the new Family Life Center that had been finished just the week before.

On entering the facility the pastor proudly stated, "And this is our newest addition to the church." The exchange student looked all around the building, not with enthusiasm, but with a look of confusion. "Well, what do you think?" the pastor finally asked

"Why didn't you give the money that it took to build all this to the poor?" the exchange student asked with a tone of disbelief. The pastor and family were silent and looked sheepishly at the ground. How would you have responded to this question?

(A copy of these case studies is available in "Teaching Resource Items" for this study at www.baptistwaypress.org.)

Encourage Application

7. Lead the class to answer questions 1 and 5 in the *Study Guide*.

8. Draw attention to the Question to Explore. Ask the class what this lesson's Scripture passage suggests. Briefly mention the tragedy of so many churches and institutions that split up and fail to accomplish the work of God. Close with a prayer for unity in God's church.

NOTES

1. Richard N. Longenecker, *Galatians*, Word Biblical Commentary, vol. 41 (Nashville and Dallas: Word Inc., 1990), 50, 51.

2. David M. Kennedy, Lizabeth Cohen, and Thomas A. Bailey, *The American Pageant, Volume II since 1865* (Boston: Houghton Mifflin Company, 13th edition, 2006), 761.

MAIN IDEA
Truly receiving the gospel transforms our social relationships, leading us to accept all the people whom God accepts.

QUESTION TO EXPLORE
What do we need to do to break down the barriers between ourselves and other Christians who seem very different from us in some way?

TEACHING AIM
To lead the group to decide on ways they will open their hearts wide to all of God's people

LESSON FOUR
One Table for God's Church

UNIT ONE
Only By Faith in Christ Jesus

BIBLE COMMENTS

Understanding the Context

The Jewish people had been set apart from the early days of the Old Testament. Monotheistic in their worship but often surrounded by hostile nations and cultures that were overwhelmingly polytheistic, the ancient Israelites struggled with their uniqueness. Often, they tainted their unique relationship with *Yahweh* by following false gods. Along the way, they also forgot they were a nation of priests to the ancient world. Ultimately, God punished them by allowing their enemies to defeat them and to carry into exile the peoples of Israel and Judah. Upon the exiles' return to Palestine to rebuild the temple, leaders like Ezra implored the Jewish people to keep themselves separate from the people of the land.

By New Testament times, conservative Jews would have absolutely nothing to do with Gentiles. Unfortunately, this attitude sometimes carried over into the New Testament church. Peter's experiences and God's call to Paul were ways in which God was working to bridge the gap that existed between Jewish Christians and the Gentile world, a gap the church had begun to close.

In this lesson's text, Paul demonstrated that the ancient prejudices against the Gentiles still existed. Despite what had occurred earlier and what Paul reported in the first part of chapter 2, some key Christian leaders backed away from fellowship with uncircumcised Gentile Christians. Consequently, Paul utilized harsh words in confronting these leaders who compromised their convictions. He recounted an event the Galatians would have remembered, and then he elaborated on why he considered it so critical that the church not succumb to the pressures of these Judaizers.

Interpreting the Scriptures

Conflict with Peter (2:11–14)

2:11. Paul recounted the story of Cephas (Peter) coming to Antioch. Antioch had a long and rich history. Because of its significance, many

Jews found their home in Antioch. By the first century AD, perhaps as many as 65,000 Jews lived in Antioch. This Jewish population probably comprised almost fifteen percent of the city's total population. Unless they had become Roman citizens, these Jews would have maintained a separate identity from other people living in and around Antioch. Apparently, the Jews at Antioch were successful in business. Their religious beliefs also attracted a number of Gentile believers who adopted at least the monotheistic elements of the Jewish faith and moral characteristics of Jewish beliefs. Subsequently, as Christianity spread to Antioch, the Christian church there became one of the most significant churches in the New Testament world. Antioch initiated the first missionary journey of Paul and Barnabas.

Because of Antioch's significance, it was no small issue when Paul confronted Peter "to his face" over his practices regarding eating with uncircumcised Gentiles. That Paul emphasized the face-to-face confrontation indicated he considered himself an equal with Peter, despite the fact that Peter's apostleship preceded his own. The verb Paul used in describing Peter's action, "stood condemned," is used only one other time in the New Testament. This verb can mean that he *stood self-condemned*. In other words, Peter's own actions condemned Peter.

2:12. What caused this confrontation? Apparently, Peter initially accepted baptized but uncircumcised Gentile Christians as equals when he came to Antioch, just as he had done with Cornelius and his household (Acts 10). However, when other Jewish Christians came from Jerusalem, Peter submitted to pressure from the Judaizers or to fear of their criticism and had nothing to do with uncircumcised Gentiles. Paul plainly stated that Peter feared the trouble these Judaizers could cause him.

2:13. Paul charged that the cowardice did not end there. Not only did Peter relent to these fears, but other Jewish Christians in Antioch, including Paul's friend and companion, Barnabas, also succumbed to pressure. Paul bluntly criticized this action as "hypocrisy." Apparently, Paul's anger erupted at such an abandonment of the gospel's freedom. In one swift swoop, he saw his work being undermined by the wavering of his fellow Jewish Christians. How could he continue to spread the gospel and overcome the already substantial barriers that existed between the

Gentiles and Jews if his fellow believers and leaders would not accept the equality offered by faith in Jesus Christ?

2:14. Paul's statement boldly answered this crisis. He told the Galatians that when he saw "that they were not straightforward about the truth of the gospel," he directly confronted Peter in front of the church. Again, as in verse 5, Paul used "the truth of the gospel" as his cornerstone. How could Peter in good conscience ask Gentiles to live like Jews, when Peter did not even live like a Jew when he was among the Gentiles? Did not the truth of the gospel demand more? Paul's problem occurred not only with the Judaizing Christians but also, and perhaps even more greatly, with those who wavered when confronted with a cultural crisis.

New Life in Grace (2:15–21)

2:15–16. Paul addressed a common prejudice that was held among both the Judaizers and Jewish Christians. They despised the moral laxity of the Gentile world. Hence, Paul used the word "sinners" to describe those from among the Gentiles. Primary reasons that Jews felt superior were their ethical system and their Old Testament law. However, Paul reminded both his hearers in Antioch and also his readers in Galatia that if Judaism and Jewish law had been enough, then Jesus' life and death would have been unnecessary. Instead, he wrote that justification now came, not from the law, but through faith in Christ. No person, said Paul, could be justified by the works of the law.

2:17–19. These verses are difficult to interpret. Paul was not debating the meaning of justification either in his discussion at Antioch or in his explanation to the Galatians. Rather, he emphasized the source of the justification. One New Testament interpreter translates this verse as, "If, at the very moment when we say that we ourselves are justified by faith alone, we turn out to be preaching to others that 'faith alone' is inadequate, but that they must keep the law as well, does that not mean that trusting in Christ is only leading them into sin? For it is teaching them not to trust the law."[1] If this translation is correct, then verses 18 and 19 are easier to understand. Paul was insisting that to return to the law, including the requirement of circumcision or any other ritual custom, meant to return to something Paul had left in the past. His experience as a believer taught him that the law had been eclipsed by the sacrifice of Christ. To return to the past destroyed the very nature of the new life in grace that Paul had experienced.

2:20–21. In verse 20, Paul spoke of one of the cornerstones of his faith. He apparently wrote the very words that he had spoken in Antioch and perhaps countless times before and after his confrontation with Peter and other Christians. When Paul stated, "I have been crucified with Christ" he utilized the perfect tense, which carried the sense that the crucifixion had not lost its power even though it occurred years earlier. By this reference, Paul also suggested that his fellow believers shared this experience with him. One commentator has suggested: "In communion with the death of Christ, the believers die to sin, so that its lordship is broken and the freedom of the life unto God is born."[2] More than this, however, Paul insisted that his life was no longer his own, and neither were his actions. The source of his life and all that flowed from it came from Christ and Christ's love. This gift of grace transcended all Paul was and did. Thus, Paul also insisted he could never "nullify the grace of God," for to do so would be to render the sacrificial death of Christ unnecessary. This would signify the depths of heresy. If believers submit themselves to the law, then the very death of Christ and its significance is at risk.

Focusing on the Meaning

Many people recognize the name of Martin Luther, the great reformer. Many of them might know that Luther is credited with starting the Protestant Reformation and beginning the Lutheran denomination. What some may not realize is what prompted Martin Luther's actions. It was not only abuses of the indulgence system or the corruption in the church Luther witnessed that motivated his actions. Part of Luther's motivation originated in his own experience. For years Luther did everything the Roman Catholic Church offered in order to try to earn his salvation. He became a monk, suffered self-denial and mortification, earned advanced degrees, studied diligently, served the church faithfully, and engaged in pilgrimages. Just like Paul, however, he found all his efforts unsatisfactory. His salvation came only when he stopped trying to earn faith and accepted the grace that God offered freely. After that, Martin Luther could not turn back to his old ways of trying to merit salvation. Ultimately, his experiences helped launch the Reformation.

In the same way, Paul rejected the attempt by the Judaizers to turn back the clock to the old Jewish ways of doing things. He recognized that the best way to spread the gospel was to break down barriers rather than erect them. He sought to accept without any restriction every person who accepted Jesus Christ. Truly, Paul recognized the image of God found in every person. He understood that Christ saved and transformed others, even the once despised Gentiles, just as Christ had saved and transformed him. Because of this he could look past previous prejudices to embrace Gentiles as brothers and sisters.

We must be careful to find the image of God in every person. We must not place restrictions on others that force them to become exactly like us as Christians before we can accept them and before they can accept Christ. Certainly, acceptance of Christ does not mean new believers are free to pursue any lifestyle they choose. As Paul wrote in another passage, "If anyone is in Christ, he is a new creature; the old things passed away; behold new things have come" (2 Corinthians 5:17). It does, however, mean that salvation is not earned. It also means that Christians must reach out to others regardless of race, ethnicity, socio-economic background, or how they look and act. As Paul worked to break down barriers with others, so must we.

TEACHING PLANS

Teaching Plan—Varied Learning Activities

Connect with Life

1. If there are more than twelve people in your class, form groups of no more than six people per group. If there are fewer than twelve people in your class, form two groups. If you have fewer than eight

people, remain as one large group. Tell the groups they have five minutes to write down on a piece of paper as many characteristics as they can that each group member shares (examples: all are parents, all live in the same city, etc.). After five minutes, have everyone come back together as a large group. Have groups share their responses. Afterward, ask:

- How did you come up with your similarities?
- What can this activity teach us about God's people?

Say: *We too often look at what makes us different from others. But when we stop and think about it, we have much in common with our brothers and sisters in Christ.*

2. Ask: *What barriers seem to keep us from forming and maintaining relationships with others?* As responses are given, write them on a board or poster. Select three responses. Ask class participants what they can do to work through each. Say: *What we are doing here is what Paul encourages us to do in today's passage: work through our barriers.*

Guide Bible Study

3. Have someone read Galatians 2:11–13 while the class listens for the situation the verses describe. Discuss the context and background of these verses, drawing from the discussion of these verses in the *Study Guide* and "Bible Comments" in this *Teaching Guide*. Especially emphasize the background of Peter's hypocrisy, as mentioned in the *Study Guide*. Ask: *How do you think Peter felt when Paul called him a hypocrite?*

4. Say: *Peter's hypocrisy was not an isolated event that just happened in his day. This scene could happen to any Christian, anytime. Let's imagine this scene happened today.* Encourage class members to come up with characters, plot, and, if time allows, dialogue for placing this scene in our day. Encourage creativity. Remind class members that the possibilities are endless. Write responses on a board. After finishing, state: *We must remember that stories like Peter's hypocrisy apply not only to biblical times but also to our day.*

Placing ourselves in the shoes of these characters helps us more fully understand biblical passages.

5. Read Galatians 2:14–21 while the class listens for the flow of Paul's comments. Either come with a prepared poster or write the following two columns and items on a board:

What You Get	What You Have to Do
• A respectful child	
• A new car	
• A promotion at work	
• A garden	

Lead the group to fill in the blanks in the "What You Have to Do" column for the corresponding items in the "What You Get" column. Challenge them to think about what the end goal ("What You Get") requires in terms of work and preparation. Then write "Salvation" under the last item in the "What You Get" column. Ask what goes under the "What You Have to Do" column for this item. State: *We assume we have to do something in order to gain things in life. But our relationship with God is different. As Paul states, we are not justified by what we do. We are justified by faith.*

6. Note that this episode is a parallel to the problems in the Galatian church, especially the Galatians following a false gospel. Refer to the introduction to unit one. Ask:
   - Why do you think Paul included this section in his letter that encouraged the Galatians to not follow a false gospel?
   - What about Paul's background gave him authority to speak about the subject of a false gospel?
   - If, like Peter, we put up barriers between ourselves and other Christians, are we somehow promoting a false gospel? Why or why not?

Encourage Application

7. Lead the class to name some divisions that exist between Christians. Ask whether they can think of things that keep Christians from engaging in warm fellowship with other Christians, especially any that seem to be most like the situation with the Galatians. Challenge class members to come up with one specific thing they can do this week to break down such barriers. Invite volunteers to share their responses.

Teaching Plan—Lecture and Questions

Connect with Life

1. Summarize the introduction to the lesson comments in the *Study Guide,* particularly the description of Paul's faithfulness. Note that biblical characters, however, also displayed unfavorable characteristics, as the "Implications and Actions" section in the *Study Guide* notes. State that Peter's actions in today's passage fit into this latter category. Say: *In this passage, Paul's uncompromising faithfulness to the gospel gave him the courage to confront Peter's hypocrisy. This challenges us to think of the ways we may shut ourselves off from accepting all people.*

Guide Bible Study

2. Have a class member read or summarize the small article "The Circumcision Group" from the *Study Guide.* Say: *The circumcision group insisted that new Christians undergo certain things with which Paul disagreed. Do you think we place any unneeded restrictions on new Christians today? If so, what?*

3. Display the outline point "The Problem (2:11–13)." Enlist a class member to read Galatians 2:11–13. Lecture on the background of Peter moving past his Jewish exclusiveness and then once again excluding Gentiles. Draw from the resources provided in this

section of the *Study Guide* and in "Bible Comments" on these verses in this *Teaching Guide*. Ask: *What groups of people do you think might feel excluded by our church?*

4. Have a different class member present each of the following case studies:

   (1) A family whose race is not well-represented at a particular church attends one of their worship services. They are greeted at the door, although not warmly, and given a worship bulletin. However, this greeting is the only words spoken to them. Much of the congregation notices the family but only nods at them in passing.

   (2) Two recently divorced women attend an adult Sunday School class at a church. The divorce of one of the women was particularly nasty and public. Therefore, most of the class members know about these women's recent history. The women are barely greeted as they enter the class and are not recognized throughout the entire class meeting.

   (A copy of the case studies is available in "Teaching Resource Items" for this study at www.baptistwaypress.org.)

   Ask:
   • What do you think about these scenarios?
   • Could either of these instances happen in our church?
   • Have you ever been made to feel like a second-class citizen at a church?
   • How do churches make people feel like second-class citizens?

5. Display the outline points "The Principle (2:14–16)" and "The Provision (2:17–21)." Enlist someone to read Galatians 2:14–21. Explain these verses by using the information in the *Study Guide* and "Bible Comments" in this *Teaching Guide*. Describe the difference between the law and the idea of justification by faith. Point out that the Galatians had accepted the good news of God's grace through the gospel. However, they were being led astray to look to the law for saving power. Encourage class members to stand firm in their commitments to Christ, looking to Paul's faithfulness as a model.

Encourage Application

6. Direct class members to the "To Apply This Lesson to Your Life" article in the *Study Guide.* Lead the class to talk about what each point means. Ask for specific ideas in applying each point to the individual lives of class members and to your local church.

7. Pass out a piece of paper and a pen to each class member. State: *The gospel transforms our social relationships, leading us to accept all the people whom God accepts. On your paper, write the first initial of one person you have a difficult time loving and accepting as he or she is.* Challenge class members to keep their papers as a reminder to accept and love that person this week. Close with prayer, asking for God's help in doing so.

NOTES

1. R. Alan Cole, *Galatians,* Tyndale New Testament Commentaries, vol. 9 (Leicester, England and Grand Rapids, MI: Inter-Varsity Press and Wm. B. Eerdmans, Publishing Co., 2nd ed., 1989), 120.

2. Herman N. Ridderbos, *The Epistle of Paul to the Churches of Galatia* (Grand Rapids, MI: Wm. B. Eerdmans Publishing Co., 1953, 1981 reprint), 105; see also 106–107.

FOCAL TEXT

Galatians 3:1–18, 26–29

BACKGROUND

Galatians 3:1–29

MAIN IDEA

Faith is the sole avenue by which we receive God's grace and are made right with God, from beginning to end.

QUESTION TO EXPLORE

What act or ritual must be added to faith in order to be related rightly to God?

TEACHING AIM

To lead the group to trace Paul's argument that faith is the sole avenue by which we are made right with God and to testify of what this truth means for their lives

LESSON FIVE

It's Faith All the Way

UNIT ONE

Only By Faith in Christ Jesus

BIBLE COMMENTS

Understanding the Context

After discussing with the Galatians his experience in Jerusalem over the conflict regarding circumcision in the previous two chapters, Paul turned his attention directly to the issue in the Galatian churches. He reminded them of their own conversions and called them back to those experiences. His initial preaching to them occurred long before any Judaizers came to Galatia. Paul wanted them to remember that their faith in Christ and not obedience to any ritual law had transformed them. In essence, Paul asked, why would they want to turn to something they had never held in the first place?

If the Galatians responded to these Judaizers who had come among them, the Galatians would be taking "a retrograde step . . . a step back from freedom to bondage, from maturity to infancy, from the status of sons to the status of servants."[1] Furthermore, as Paul reminded them, when they became Christians they experienced evidences of the Spirit in their lives. The Spirit would continue to mold and transform them into people who were guided by God's Spirit and not by the sinful desires of their past.

After this plea, Paul reminded his readers of the Old Testament purposes behind the law. At this point, he referred to God's covenant with Abraham. Essentially, Paul insisted that the Mosaic Law came after the Abrahamic covenant but did not invalidate it. In the same way, Paul regarded the promise of redemption through Christ as a fulfillment of both God's promise to Abraham and the Mosaic Law. As he wrote in Galatians 3:24, "the Law has become our tutor to lead us to Christ."

Interpreting the Scriptures

Paul's Struggle Against Legalism (3:1–18)

3:1. Paul used rich imagery in this verse. He utilized rhetorical devices that various public speakers in that era commonly employed. His writing took the form of questions that challenged the thought processes of his readers. First, Paul called the Galatians "foolish." He used the same word again in verse 3. His choice of words revealed how concerned Paul had become. While he undoubtedly called the Galatians "foolish" because he was frustrated with them, their behavior clearly baffled him. Paul could not understand how they could so lack spiritual insight.

A second strong word Paul employed was "bewitched." This word can also be translated as *fascinated*. This is the only time this Greek word is used in the entire New Testament. Paul suggested that the Judaizers who misled the Galatians completely mesmerized them with their arguments. Paul could not understand how the Galatians could fall for such tactics. After all, Paul himself had openly shared with them the core of the gospel. He did not hide the truth of Christ's atoning death behind mysteries or in secret rituals. He proclaimed the crucified Christ "publicly."

3:2–3. Paul cut immediately to the heart of the matter. Once again using a question, he interrogated his readers. He was asking them if they had received the Spirit because of their faith or because they continued to adhere to the law. Of course, Paul knew the answer to this question, but he used this rhetorical device to cause them to think about what they were doing. He knew that the gifts of the Spirit had come upon them once they declared their faith and not later when the Judaizers had misled them.

"Hearing with faith" might also be understood as *believing the message of faith*.[2] Paul used this same expression in verse 5. Clearly Paul stressed that belief was more important than an outward observance of some kind. In verse 3 he called the Galatians "foolish" again. Why would they adopt a ritual observance once the Spirit had fallen upon them?

3:4. Verse 4 could refer to a couple of things. It is possible that Paul referred to some suffering that the Galatian Christians had experienced as a result of the persecution similar to those he had experienced in Acts 14. It is also possible, however, to translate this passage: *have you had such wonderful spiritual experiences all to no purpose?* Such a translation fits better with what Paul had said about the work of the Holy Spirit in verses 2 and 3.

3:5. Paul elaborated on the concept advanced in verse 3 by referring again to the Holy Spirit. He stated that God "provides" believers with the Spirit. This word can be translated as *grants, gives,* or *supports.* The Spirit also "works miracles" in the believer's life. Paul rhetorically asked the Galatians whether these miracles came through the law or through faith. To Paul the answer was obvious—through faith.

3:6–7. The Apostle referenced Abraham, the great patriarch of the faith. He quoted an Old Testament passage, Genesis 15:6, to illustrate that Abraham's faith counted as the source of his righteousness. Those who are saved by faith are descendants of Abraham as were the Jews who insisted on keeping the law. Paul utilized that idea to contradict the claim that Jewish customs must be followed for one to become a Christian. The key was, and is, faith.

3:8–9. Having introduced Abraham as his illustration, Paul linked Scripture's foreknowledge that God would "justify the Gentiles by faith" to the message given to Abraham that "all nations will be blessed in you." Paul contended that faith, not external rights, was the key to their gaining salvation. These Galatian Gentiles were Abraham's descendants by faith.

3:10–12. In these verses, Paul returned to the concept of living under the authority of the Old Testament law. Paul once again strongly and directly attacked the Judaizers' claims. He contrasted those living under the law with those under faith by referencing Scripture (Deuteronomy 27:26; Habakkuk 2:4). In essence, Paul demonstrated that these two passages, which were those most likely used by the Judaizers, only mention the law in relationship to a curse. By contrast, where faith is mentioned so is righteousness. In other words, faith in Jesus as the Messiah lifted the curse of the law and extended Abraham's blessing to the Gentiles and gave the Holy Spirit to the Galatians. Thus, verses 10 and 12 parallel each other. Verse 11 stands between them as a contrast.

3:13–14. Paul wrote that "Christ redeemed" believers. "Redeemed" can be literally translated as *bought back* or *bought out of* in the same way that a soldier might have purchased release from the army or a slave purchased freedom from slavery. Paul said that the law necessitated such redemption. As such, Jesus became a curse that it might be possible for Gentiles to become recipients of both the Abrahamic blessing and then to receive God's Holy Spirit through faith.

3:15–16. Paul began here to discuss the intent of the law. He illustrated by suggesting that even among human beings, once a covenant was established, it was considered a binding agreement, and new conditions could not be added. Paul's declaration was important because of his statement in verse 16. He argued that the promises God made were to Abraham and "his seed." He interpreted this to mean the "seed" that God referred to with Abraham was Jesus Christ.

3:17–18. Having established the historical foundation, Paul came to his major purpose. As covenants made by people are binding and cannot be voided by additions, even more so are covenants made between God and humanity. Paul argued that God's promise to Abraham pre-dated that of the Mosaic Law by hundreds of years and was not invalidated by it. God's promise was more than adequate through all those years without any sort of law. He further argued that Abraham's inheritance could not be based on law because it is based on God's promise. In other words, Paul insisted that God's promise made to Abraham and fulfilled in Christ trumped the law.

Paul's Call for Unity Through Faith (3:26–29)

3:26–27. Paul closed this section of his letter with these summary statements. First, he maintained that everyone who expresses faith in Christ Jesus is a child of God. He used imagery that compared baptism with clothing. Another way of interpreting this is to say that believers put on a relationship with Christ that is symbolized in baptism.

3:28–29. The ritual law of circumcision existed only for males. God's promise, however, extends to everyone, be they slave or free, Jew or Gentile, male or female. Race and culture, status of servitude, and gender all pass away in the unity that comes through Jesus Christ. This does not mean that these differences do not exist. They are still present. However, Paul said that salvation by faith is open to everyone without regard for class, ethnicity, gender, or social differences. The inheritance of faith that began in Abraham has been completed by faith in Jesus Christ. It calls to mind also the earlier statement that Paul made in Ephesians 2:14, "For He Himself is our peace who made both groups into one and broke down the barrier of the dividing wall."

Focusing on the Meaning

Pressured by the Judaizers to accept Jewish customs and rituals in order to be in right relationship with God, the Galatian Christians faced a serious question: were they to minimize the importance of faith in order to be accepted by those who criticized the way Paul taught? Paul's answer to them reverberated throughout this part of the letter. The only true way to right relationship with God is faith in Jesus Christ.

Today's Christian faces a constant temptation to try to validate the Christian experience through custom and ritual or through following a set of laws. There is a very human tendency to fail to trust in faith alone. Over and over again, humans have sought to add something else to the gospel. In some cases it might be to insist on a certain form of worship or to follow the entreaties of a charismatic leader. In other cases, it might be compulsory church attendance or adoption of a particular brand of denomination. In yet other cases it might be compulsory financial participation or maintaining a certain ethical code. The bottom line of what Paul was arguing for in chapter 3 is that there is no replacement for faith. While it is important for believers to live sound moral lives, to worship regularly, and to participate in a local congregation, including financially supporting it, these should be reflections of our faith, not methods of earning salvation.

Beyond this, what we need to hear today is that Paul stressed that there are no dividing lines or classifications of Christians. All who trust in Jesus Christ are one.

TEACHING PLANS

Teaching Plan—Varied Learning Activities

Connect with Life

1. Ask class members how they did with the challenge at the end of lesson four (see the final step in either "Teaching Plan—Varied Learning Activities" or "Teaching Plan—Lecture and Questions"). Invite follow-up questions or thoughts. Note that this lesson builds on lesson four and further explores the idea of justification by faith alone.

2. Ask:
   - How have your thoughts and beliefs about God changed since you were a child?
   - What causes people to re-think their thoughts and beliefs?

   State: *In today's passage, Paul encouraged the Galatian Christians to re-think their thoughts and beliefs. Paul's words were harsh and urgent. He not only wanted the Galatians to change their thoughts. He scolded them and told them to not abandon the gospel he preached to them.*

Guide Bible Study

3. Have a class member read Galatians 3:1–5 while the class listens for the questions Paul asked and the tone in them. Receive reports. (See "Questions About God's Plan" in the *Study Guide* for help in identifying and explaining the questions.) Emphasize that Paul was shocked and amazed that the Galatians turned their back on their faith in Christ. State: *The word "bewitched" in verse 1 means that the Galatians were put under the spell of the Judaizers, those who were leading them astray.*

4. Divide the class into groups of three to six people each (unless you have fewer than six people, in which case remain as one group).

Have each group come up with a short skit (between one and two minutes long) that shows an example of how we, too, can be bewitched in our faith. Allow groups a couple of minutes to design their skits. Then have each group perform their skit for the larger group.

Afterward, ask: *How do Paul's words in Galatians 3:1–5 apply to these modern-day examples of being led astray in one's faith?*

5. Enlist someone to read Galatians 3:6–18 while the class listens for Paul's flow of thought in his comments about Abraham. State: *In these verses, we learn that from the beginning, God intended for faith, not the law, to be primary in a person's rightly relating to God. Paul used Old Testament references to show that even when the Israelites lived under the law, God desired obedience through faith from them. Therefore, faith fulfills God's promises given to Abraham and others throughout the Old Testament.*

6. Have the class again form the groups used in step 4. Assign each group the task of teaching a Bible study lesson on Galatians 3:6–18 to new adult Christians in your church. The main point they are trying to teach is that faith in Christ fulfills God's promises of the Old Testament. Tell the groups they may use any teaching method(s) they choose. Be sure to have them apply the lesson to everyday life. Refer them to "A Historical Example of God's Plan" in the *Study Guide* for help in understanding and explaining the verses. Allow the class four or five minutes to come up with overviews of their lessons. Then have each group present their overview in two or three minutes to the larger group. Ask: *Was this task easy or difficult?* Say: *Thinking about teaching Bible lessons can help us better understand them for ourselves.*

7. Have four class members read each verse of Galatians 3:26–29. See whether a class member who wears glasses or contacts can remember what it was like to try on his or her first pair of prescription glasses. Have the person share that experience with the class. Or, share your own experience with the class. Note that this experience is similar to what Paul described in this passage.

8. State: *As Christians, Jesus changes our outlook on life. Salvation transforms every part of our lives, including our thoughts, beliefs,*

attitudes, words, and actions. In verse 26, Paul described three barriers between people of his day: social, ethnic, and gender. He tells us that as Christians, we need to change our lives so that these differences no longer matter. Ask: *How do these barriers still exist today? What other barriers do we struggle with today?*

Encourage Application

9. Direct class members to the "To Apply This Lesson to Your life" article in the *Study Guide*. Ask whether any points specifically apply to the lives of class members. Focus on each point, and ask for specific ways each can be applied to their lives and to their church.

Teaching Plan—Lecture and Questions

Connect with Life

1. Ask whether anyone has any follow-up thoughts about the previous session's challenge to love and accept a specific person (see the final step in either "Teaching Plan—Varied Learning Activities" or "Teaching Plan—Lecture and Questions").

2. Lead class members to think of a time when someone did not express gratitude for the help the person received. In advance, think of an example in case no one is able to offer one, preferably a personal illustration. State: *Just as we can be ungrateful for help, the Galatians lost their appreciation for God's gift of salvation through Christ. They tried to take over their own faith and Christian growth. We also must remember the Christian life not only begins with faith but also that Christian growth continues with faith and faithfully looks forward to heaven—it's faith all the way.*

Guide Bible Study

3. Display the outline point "Questions About God's Plan (3:1–5)." Invite someone to read Galatians 3:1–5. In advance, ask a class

member to prepare a brief report (two-to-three minutes) on who the Judaizers were and what requirements they placed on the Galatians. After the presentation, say: *This was the context in which Paul wrote today's passage. Paul pleaded with the Galatians not to place their faith in rituals, like circumcision. He said these things could not confirm their experience of faith in Christ. We do not need to add anything to faith to have a right relationship with God.*

4. Display the outline point "A Historical Example of God's Plan (3:6–18)." Have a class member read Galatians 3:6–18. Summarize the section "Abraham" in the *Study Guide.*

5. Say: *Abraham understood God's covenant as being through faith, not through rituals. The ritual of circumcision came after Abraham's acceptance by faith of God's call. Paul also called the Galatians to understand that faith in Christ is available to all people, not just those who undergo circumcision. Paul also called the Galatians to look to Abraham as an example of true faith in God.* Ask: *What can Abraham's life teach us about faith?*

6. Display this outline point: "The Result of God's Plan (3:26–29)." Then display these words on a markerboard or a poster:

Three Common Barriers in Biblical Times

- Ethnicity
- Social class
- Gender

Have someone read Galatians 3:26–29 while the class listens for these three barriers. Comment: *Circumcision was available only to males. Therefore, in these verses, Paul told the Galatians that true faith in Christ is available to all people, regardless of human barriers.* Referring to the poster, say: *These barriers still exist today. Our faith in Christ cannot eliminate these barriers. But with God, these differences no longer matter. What can we do to be sure these differences do not matter in our daily lives?*

Encourage Application

7. State: *We are not perfect and cannot help but be tempted to set up barriers between ourselves and others. But, we must remember that as Christians, God wants us to do our best. We are on a journey. Salvation is a process on which we always rely on God by faith. It is not just a one-time experience, and it never is based on our works, as the Galatians were tempted to believe.*

8. Encourage class members to think about their faith journeys. Have them close their eyes, bow their heads, and spend a few moments in silence as they choose an area of their faith development that is particularly lacking and needs attention. Offer examples, such as regularly reading the Bible or forgiving someone. Close with prayer, asking for God's help.

NOTES

1. F. F. Bruce, *Paul, Apostle of the Heart Set Free* (Grand Rapids, MI: William B. Eerdmans Publishing, 1977, 1986), 182.

2. See Richard Hays, "The Letter to the Galatians," *The New Interpreter's Bible*, vol. XI (Nashville: Abingdon Press, 2000), on Galatians 3:2.

FOCAL TEXT
Galatians 4:1–10; 5:1

BACKGROUND
Galatians 4:1—5:1

MAIN IDEA
When we come to know
God by faith, God frees us
from whatever binds us to
live fully as his children.

QUESTION TO EXPLORE
To what extent have you
accepted your freedom to live
life fully as a child of God?

TEACHING AIM
To lead adults to describe
the life of being set free to
be a child of God by faith in
contrast to life otherwise

LESSON SIX
Set Free to Be
God's Children

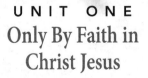

UNIT ONE
Only By Faith in
Christ Jesus

BIBLE COMMENTS

Understanding the Context

Galatians 4 continues many of the same thoughts Paul presented in chapter 3. While English Bibles have chapter breaks, these were added centuries after Paul originally wrote the letter. At times, chapter breaks may cloud the continuity between chapters. Paul was persisting in his discussion of the Galatians being led astray by the Judaizers' insistence on being circumcised and keeping the Mosaic Law.

Most of the Galatian Christians had converted from paganism. They had never lived under Jewish law. In fact, they most likely were not monotheistic but were polytheistic. The only law that would have concerned them would have been Roman law. Thus, Paul continued in his arguments against any turning—not returning since they had never observed Jewish customs—to Jewish ritual. This passage further illustrates how revolutionary Paul's thinking had become. Before Paul met Christ on the Damascus road, any such rejection of Jewish law, custom, or ritual would have been impossible for Paul. But as chapter 4 demonstrates, Paul, while still retaining his Jewish character, had jettisoned any reliance on the law for his salvation. The gospel had freed him completely from his past.

Interpreting the Scriptures

Not Slaves But Children (4:1–7)

4:1–2. Paul named four different types of people—heirs, fathers, guardians, and stewards ("managers"). "Managers" might be translated as *governors*. Law in the ancient world established that, if the father died, the heir would be supervised by guardians and stewards. If the father died before the child came of age, responsibility for the child passed to the guardian, usually until the age of fourteen. Then responsibility passed to a steward who managed the heir's affairs until about the age of twenty-five. It did not matter the size of the estate, the heir would be essentially a slave even though the heir stood to inherit all. The heir was bound by this arrangement until the date established by the father. Paul used the father-child relationship to pick up on the concept that believers are "sons of God" (Galatians 3:26).

4:3. Paul used the previous verses as an example of the bondage experienced by the Galatians. In the same way, Paul said that "we"—grouping himself with the Galatians at this point, despite his different ethnic background—were held in bondage as well. What Paul conveyed was that while acknowledging that they all had once been infants or children, now they were no longer young but had matured because of their experience of faith. Why, then, should they revert to spiritual childhood and to the bondage of inheritance they once had felt?

4:4–5. Verse 4 is one of the most powerful verses in the entire Bible. "The fullness of the time" demonstrates that God works in time to accomplish divine purposes. God determined the exact time for the first coming of Christ. Paul also said that "God sent forth His Son." "Sent forth" can mean *sent forth on a mission*, a derivative of the word for apostleship. Paul sought to connect his apostleship with the mission of Christ by using these words. The intensity of the conflict in the Galatian churches apparently made Paul highly conscious of his need to speak authoritatively.

"Born of a woman" may accomplish two purposes. By writing this, Paul addressed Jesus' full humanity. The phrase might also be an allusion to the virgin birth. The last phrase of the verse, "under the law," was yet another allusion to the controversy he was addressing. Verse 5 completes the sentence. The purpose of Jesus' mission was to redeem those who were born under the law. This redemption led to the adoption of Paul, the Galatians, and us as God's children.

4:6–7. Countless arguments have been raised about the sequence of which comes first, adoption and then the Holy Spirit or the Holy Spirit and then adoption. But perhaps Paul was not concerned at this point with "stages in the Christian life," but instead was concerned about "reciprocal relation or the correlational nature of sonship and the reception of the Spirit."[1] The phrase "into our hearts" means the association Paul made regarding the idea of having Christ in us. The intimate terms

"Abba, Father" refer to God. What Paul did was to teach that, once the Holy Spirit resided in these Galatian Christians, they could address God directly and intimately. "Therefore" indicates that, because of what he had been saying, the heirs resided no longer in bondage but were full heirs of the promises of God. Children cannot truly be slaves. If the Galatians were God's children, they were also God's heirs of salvation.

Not gods but God (4:8–10)

4:8. Paul provided his readers with another contrast. He used a common Jewish literary device to do so. He said that the Galatians once "did not know God" but worshiped gods that were not real. His words indicated a common concern about the Gentiles—their polytheistic culture. The absurdity of worshiping things humans created with their own hands rather than worshiping the Creator appalled a devout Jew.

4:9. The biblical meaning of the word "know" is far greater than intellectual or head knowledge. In the Bible, "know" can mean heart knowledge and an intimacy that goes beyond intellectual assent. "Know" carries the meaning of a bond that transcends mere mental awareness. Paul clarified this further by changing his wording to say that Christians were "known by God." Given that intimacy, Paul asked, how could they return to a bondage to "the weak and worthless" things of the world? While this return might not have been intentional on their parts, to Paul it became the logical outcome of their decision should they continue to follow the Judaizers.

4:10. This verse seems to be an indication that the Galatians had adopted the Jewish liturgical calendar along with other Jewish customs and ritual. So not only had the Galatians adopted food laws and circumcision (Gal. 2:12) but also the ritual observances and calendar.

Stand Firm (5:1)

Paul apparently agonized over this situation with the Galatians. He probably worried that so much of what he had fought for in the preceding years would be wasted if the Galatians continued to follow after the Judaizers. The remainder of chapter 4 continued his arguments and illustrations. As the next chapter begins, Paul summarized these arguments and illustrations with a powerful statement: "It was for freedom that Christ set us free." Paul emphatically declared this.

Christ did not set believers free to resume slavery in another form. Thus, Paul implored his readers to "stand firm." This may have been one of Paul's favorite phrases. It can be found often in his writing (1 Corinthians 16:13; Ephesians 6:13; Philippians 1:27; 1 Thessalonians 3:8). The Galatians must "stand firm" in freedom and refuse any legalistic attempts to restore any sort of bondage. To accept subjugation to the law would be to render vain the work of Christ for them.

Focusing on the Meaning

In the summer of 1862, Abraham Lincoln found himself tremendously burdened. For some time, he had believed that merely fighting to preserve the Union was not enough. Despite the fact that he had insisted since the beginning of America's Civil War that the war was not being fought to end slavery but to put down the rebellion in the southern states, he recognized the need to lift the war to a higher cause. That summer he presented to his cabinet the first draft of a document that attempted to do this. They largely approved of the document but opposed the timing. They feared that, due to the poor fortunes of the Union war effort in the eastern theater, issuing a controversial proclamation might smack of desperation. They urged him to wait for a Union victory.

That victory came in September of 1862 at Antietam Creek in Maryland. There Union forces turned back the Confederate invasion of the North. After the victory, President Lincoln issued his famous Emancipation Proclamation declaring "on the first day of January, in the year of our Lord one thousand eight hundred and sixty-three, all persons held as slaves within any State or designated part of a State, the people whereof shall then be in rebellion against the United States, shall be then, thenceforward, and forever free."[2] This document changed the nature of the war, creating what Lincoln later described as a "new birth of freedom." Validated with the passage and ratification of the Thirteenth Amendment to the Constitution and with Union victory in 1865, almost four million African Americans found themselves officially free from bondage. Finally, the United States could begin to live up to the promise of the Declaration of Independence that "all men are created equal." Finally, African Americans could experience the *Year of Jubilee* or the *Exodus* for which they had prayed so long. In the months that followed, these newly liberated men and women sought to enjoy their newfound freedom in numerous ways. They were free!

In similar fashion, Paul was telling the Galatians and telling us that we are free. We must accept this freedom. We cannot be bound by legalistic restrictions that might cause us to be in bondage to custom, ritual observance, or senseless tradition. Custom, ritual, and tradition all have uses and often benefits, but they are not the means to salvation. Freedom always comes with a price—in this case, a price that Jesus paid. Freedom also carries responsibility. That responsibility is for us to stand firm in our faith. Paul would later in the letter describe what that responsibility means for the believer as he discussed the practical Christian life and community.

TEACHING PLANS

Teaching Plan—Varied Learning Activities

Connect with Life

1. Have class members close their eyes and sit comfortably in their chairs. Lead them through a story that helps them imagine the experience of being unshackled, set free from some sort of bondage or enslavement. Be creative. Help them see and feel the situation. A story example is available in "Teaching Resource Items" for this study at www.baptistwaypress.org.

2. Ask:
   - How did that feel?
   - Describe the experience of being set free.
   - How does this experience compare to the Christian life?

Say: *When we come to know God by faith in Christ, we gain freedom. The Christians in Galatia also found freedom in Christ. But, as we have learned in the previous lessons on Galatians, they turned their back on this freedom. In this Scripture passage, Paul encouraged them to be strong in threats against this freedom.*

Guide Bible Study

3. Have a class member read Galatians 4:1–7 while the class listens for the images Paul used to describe God's provision of freedom. After the reading, ask: *How did Paul describe our status as Christians in this passage?* State: *The freedom we have in Christ is a privilege. We gain this privilege as we come to know God by faith, just as the heir was no longer considered a child, even a slave, until receiving the inheritance. We also have privileges in our lives when a change of status occurs.*

4. Ask the class for examples of privileges that come about from status changes. Write them on the left side of a board or poster, under the heading "Privilege." After you have four or five privileges, ask them what responsibilities go with each privilege. Write responses on the right side of the board, under the heading "Responsibilities." Some examples are listed below:

Privilege	Responsibility
Driver's license	
Ability to vote	
Living on your own	

Then, write "Freedom in Christ" under the last item in the "Privilege" column. Ask what goes under the "Responsibilities" column for this item. Say: *With our privileges come responsibilities. We must remember that as Christians, God frees us from whatever binds us. This means, though, that we have a responsibility to live as children of God.*

5. Enlist someone to read Galatians 4:8–10 while the class listens for why Paul was concerned about the Galatians. Ask: *What was Paul trying to tell the Galatians in this passage?* State: *Today's passage shows us that freedom in Christ sets us free to live differently than we have before.* Have a class member read verse 10 again. Explain the context and specific meaning of this verse using information in the *Study Guide* and "Bible Comments" in this *Teaching Guide*. Note that just as the Galatians held onto these Jewish rituals, we, too, may hold on to cultural practices and our former ways of living. Call for specific examples. Provide further insights as seems helpful from "A Word of Warning (4:8–10)" in the *Study Guide*.

6. Read Galatians 5:1 by having class members each say one word of the verse until it is completed. Use the Scripture translation in the *Study Guide* so that all will have the same translation. Point out that our freedom in Christ frees us *from* certain things and also frees us *for* new life as children of God. Elaborate on this truth with information from the *Study Guide*. Connect this idea with the story you use in step 1 (this story also describes a freedom *from* something and a freedom *for* something).

7. Lead class members to name things our freedom in Christ frees us *for*. Write responses on a board. Call for specific ways (and include your own) to put these things into action in the life of a child of God.

Encourage Application

8. State: *When we do not follow recipes correctly, our food does not taste as good. Or when we fail to follow the directions when trying to assemble something, it may turn out not working or not looking like what was intended. Our lives are also less than they should be when we do not live up to our freedom in Christ.* Divide the class into groups of three to six people each (unless there are fewer than six people, in which case remain as one group). Pass out paper and pens. Have each group come up with a recipe or directions for *living fully as a child of God*. Encourage groups to think about how living fully as a child of God is different from living by relying on other alternatives such as cultural practices and religious rituals. After

about five minutes, have the groups come back together as a large group and share their thoughts. Encourage the class to live up to their freedom in Christ.

Teaching Plan—Lecture and Questions

Connect with Life

1. In advance, enlist a class member to prepare a presentation (three-to-five minutes) on the story of Bertha Adams, as mentioned in the introduction to the lesson in the *Study Guide*.

2. Ask:
   * How do you feel about this story?
   * Why do you think this person chose to live beneath the level of her resources?
   * How can Christians sometimes be like this person?

   State: *The Galatian Christians were doing something similar. The Galatians were living beneath their spiritual resources. Sadly, we too often do the same thing. As we study this Scripture together, think about how we do that.*

Guide Bible Study

3. Display the outline point "Before Christ Comes (4:1–3)." Have a class member read Galatians 4:1–3 while the class listens for the comparison Paul was making. Explain the context of Jewish family life as described in this passage, using information in the *Study Guide* and "Bible Comments" in this *Teaching Guide*. Ask: *If Paul were making his point in our day, what illustration do you think he might use?*

4. Display the outline point "After Christ Comes (4:4–7)." Have a class member read Galatians 4:4–7. State: *These verses tell us that Jesus completely provides for us. Since Jesus is both fully God and fully human, Jesus knows exactly what it is like to be in our shoes. For that reason, Jesus can sympathize with and understand us and our*

situations. Elaborate on Jesus restoring our full privileges as children of God, using the information in the *Study Guide* and "Bible Comments" in this *Teaching Guide.*

5. Display the outline point "A Word of Warning (4:8–10)." Have a class member read Galatians 4:8–10 while the class listens for Paul's response to what the Galatian Christians were doing. State: *Paul compared the Galatians' lives at that time with their lives before knowing Christ. He basically said their faith in Christ was no longer meaning anything to them because of their return to relying on rituals and cultural practices. This is a harsh statement! Paul stressed two things to which the Galatians were turning back: ignorance and enslavement.* Add information from the *Study Guide* and "Bible Comments" in this *Teaching Guide.* Then ask:

   - How can we be ignorant in our faith?
   - What can enslave us as Christians?

6. Display the outline point "A Challenge to Claim Their Freedom (5:1)." Enlist someone to read Galatians 5:1 while the class listens for Paul's instruction to the Galatians. Say: *Going back to our old way of doing things can sometimes be comfortable. That is what we know and are used to. Paul said that when we do this, we live beneath our privileges, beneath our spiritual resources.* Ask class members to name ways we sometimes live beneath our privileges of faith in Christ. List responses on a board.

Encourage Application

7. Refer to and ask questions 1 and 5 in the *Study Guide.* Have a different class member read each question. Encourage class members to apply the answers to their lives.

8. Pass out a note card and a pen or pencil to each class member. Say: *Identifying what holds us back from full freedom in Christ is important. No matter where we are on our Christian journeys, we can always work on something. Take a few moments to think of one thing that is currently holding you back.* Allow class members one to two minutes to write something down. Then, encourage everyone to keep the note card with them this week as a reminder to work on

what they have written. Invite a class member to close the session in prayer.

NOTES

1. Richard N. Longenecker, *Galatians,* Word Biblical Commentary, vol. 41 (Nashville and Dallas: Word Inc., 1990), 173–175.

2. http://showcase.netins.net/web/creative/lincoln/speeches/ emancipate.htm. Accessed 4/17/2009.

FOCAL TEXT
Galatians 5:13–26

BACKGROUND
Galatians 5:2–26

MAIN IDEA
Not keeping the law but living by God's Spirit enables God's people to love others and show in their lives the fruit of the Spirit rather than the works of the flesh.

QUESTION TO EXPLORE
Is living by God's Spirit rather than keeping the law sufficient to keep us on the right track in life?

TEACHING AIM
To lead the class to contrast life in the Spirit to fulfilling the desires of the flesh and evaluate their lives by the qualities of life in the Spirit

LESSON SEVEN

Walk By the Spirit

UNIT TWO
The Gospel in Life

BIBLE COMMENTS

Understanding the Context

Paul used a similar approach in writing many of his letters to New Testament churches. Typically, he laid out his theological arguments in the first portion of the letter. Then, usually in the latter half or third of his epistle, he would make the transition to an ethical application of the theological arguments he had made. He often signaled this with a word like "therefore" (Colossians 3:1; 2 Corinthians 7:1; Ephesians 4:1). While he didn't utilize such a transitional word or phrase in today's text, the transition does exist. Chapters 5 and 6 mark a shift to ethical application. These chapters are closely linked to the preceding portions of the letter.

Paul offered two ethical lessons. First, he insisted that freedom in Christ was not license to sin. Second, he stressed that ethical behavior, while not a prerequisite to salvation, occurred where true salvation existed. Ethics and faith went hand-in-hand for Paul, much as it did for Paul's contemporary, James.

Interpreting the Scriptures

The Law of Love (5:13–15)

5:13–14. After one final warning against legalism in the first part of this chapter (5:2–12), Paul laid out the standard for the Christian life. Paul implored the Galatians to respond to the freedom they received in Christ, not by giving in to the flesh, but by being free to serve. Apparently, the Judaizing Christians believed that once people had been set free by God's grace through Christ, the high ethical standards of Judaism would be lost. Instead, Paul insisted that freedom should not be understood as freedom for the flesh to do what it wants but rather as an opportunity for service. Their freedom could be employed to serve others. Indeed, as he wrote in verse 14, the whole law can be summed up in this quotation from Leviticus 19:18, "You shall love your neighbor as yourself."

The Galatian Christians would have been aware that Jesus himself, when responding to the questioning by the Pharisees as to the greatest commandment, quoted the passage in Leviticus as well as Deuteronomy 6:5. The law of love and service eclipsed the injunctions in Leviticus and Deuteronomy for Paul. As one commentator explains, "The law is and remains for him also an expression of the will of God. . . . He does not bind believers to the law in the concrete and historical form" of the law but in "the command of love, in which the whole law has its summary and fulfillment."[1] These verses fit perfectly with what Paul wrote in the preceding chapters.

5:15. In this verse, Paul painted a word picture not unlike saying *if you fight like cats and dogs* or like portraying wild animals fighting to the death. Another image is of two snakes grabbing each other by the tail until they swallow each other.

Perhaps the Galatians were fighting over what the Judaizers were suggesting. Or perhaps Paul was referring to those who used the gift of grace to engage in excessive and unchristian conduct. Either way, Paul minced no words in dealing with this extreme behavior by the Galatians just as he had dealt with that of the Judaizers.

Life in the Spirit (5:16–26)

5:16–18. The presence of the Holy Spirit in believers' lives becomes the distinguishing mark for Christians. The role of the Spirit in Paul's ethical commentary is unique. The following verses build on this theme. First, Paul exhorted: "Walk by the Spirit." He connected this exhortation to a promise. If the Galatians would "walk by the Spirit," in turn he could promise that they would "not carry out the desire of the flesh." Essentially, Paul argued that there is a spiritual contest between the carnal behavior of humans and the presence of the Spirit. The Spirit acts as a counterweight to fleshly desires. The struggle can be compared to a tug of war. This passage might also be compared with Paul's writing in Romans 7 in which he spoke of doing things he did not wish to do. He also failed to behave in more positive ways that he also felt were important. Furthermore, whereas the law once served to counteract the desires of the flesh, now the Holy Spirit does so.

5:19–21. Generally, some commentators believe these verses that describe life in the flesh are to be contrasted to the life in the Spirit (5:22–23). Paul might have been referring to some sort of traditional list of sins or vices in this passage. Some writers suggest that this is a random collection, while others suggest Paul listed a catalogue of vices that can be classified in groups. Three deal with various forms of sexual sin. Two address forms of pagan religious practices. Eight relate to interpersonal relationships and conflict while the final two relate to alcohol abuse and what can result from that.

The first set, sexual sins, is translated or interpreted in different fashions. The word translated "immorality" is the root word of our word *pornography.* Some writers believe the word refers to prostitution. Others believe it can be translated as *fornication* and refers to any sexual irregularities while "impurity" and "sensuality" are more specific. Paul might have used these two latter words to refer to sexual perversions such as he discussed in Romans 1:26–27. "Sensuality" may also be interpreted to mean *lack of restraint.*

The second set of vices, "idolatry" and "sorcery," indicate how strong competing religions were in Paul's time. "Sorcery" may also be translated as *witchcraft,* an especially reprehensible act in the Old Testament context (Deuteronomy 18:10, 14). Paul was reminding the Galatians of the dangers of these competing religious views that corrupted spiritual life.

The third set of vices relate to relational sins or "sins of the spirit." "Enmities" most likely means *personal animosities* while "strife" can be understood as *rivalry* or *discord.* Paul listed "jealousy" and "outbursts of anger" next. "Jealousy" can be translated as plural, *jealousies,* with the suggestion that it was directed toward more than one person. "Outbursts of anger" suggests an emotional outburst or explosion.

The final four of these vices, "disputes, dissensions, factions, envying," deal with problems that can be translated as *party spirit, splits in two, preferences,* and *feelings of ill will.* While on the surface these latter vices may not seem as harmful as some of the preceding ones, anyone who has endured a church split or been on the outside of a clique will verify the destructive nature of these vices in a church.

The final set of spiritual sins or vices Paul addressed contain "drunkenness" and "carousing." The Roman world had acquired the reputation of rampant problems of alcohol abuse, although the Gentile culture of that day might have been no worse than either previous or recent cultures.

Paul concluded his description of these vices by insisting that those who practiced these types of sin would "not inherit the kingdom of God." At first glance, it might appear that Paul contradicted himself. He had argued for salvation by grace and now seemed to suggest that the practice of these sins would bar these individuals from God's kingdom. However, Paul was being consistent. As the next two verses demonstrate, Paul verified that those who truly have experienced God's grace and are led by the Spirit will not engage in habitual practice of these vices but will exhibit "the fruit of the Spirit" rather than the "deeds of the flesh." He was simply reminding the Galatians of what their lives were like before they encountered Christ.

5:22–23. These verses contrast the life in the Spirit to life in the flesh and should not be taken as a command or as a prerequisite to living in the Spirit. Rather the fruit grows out of life in the Spirit. Paul meant the verses to be descriptive of the results of the Spirit-filled life. The metaphor, "fruit," was a common one to agricultural people and one with which the Galatians would have been familiar. Fruit was most often used to describe the produce of the tree or the vine. Paul did not use the gifts of the Spirit as proof of the Galatians' experience as he had done in other letters. Certainly, the indication is that the fruit of the Spirit is a spontaneous result of the Spirit's presence in believers' lives. The whole list implies that the harvest of God's presence in Christians is these characteristics.

The word Paul used for "love" is the word we find in the New Testament most often used for Christian or godly love. It generally described sacrificing, self-giving love. It needs little further description except to acknowledge that Paul began his list with the most important fruit of all. From it all the other fruit are harvested. "Joy" and "peace" are variations on the words often used in Jewish-Christian greetings and with which Paul often began his letters.

"Patience" may also be translated as *tolerance* or *long-temperedness* in contrast to *short-temperedness*. It might also be understood to contrast the "outbursts of anger" Paul cited as indication of life in the flesh. "Kindness" carries the idea of *goodness* or *generosity*. Non-Christians may have ridiculed these believers as *goodie-goodies*. We know that throughout Christianity's history, Christians have often been mocked as *do-gooders.* "Goodness" probably has more of a meaning of *generosity* rather than service. Obviously, these last four fruit are directed more towards fellow humans than God. "Faithfulness" could mean faith toward God. However, if it is grouped with the previous four and the following two that are qualities directed toward other humans, Paul probably intended it to mean something more akin to *fidelity* or *loyalty.*

The fruit "gentleness" might be accurately translated as *humility,* especially if it is considered in light of "kindness" and "goodness." "Self-control," unlike the preceding fruit, is more of an inward quality than an outward quality. This would be consistent if Paul were reprimanding those in Galatia who, in contrast to the strict legalists, were using the freedom in Christ and God's grace as license to sin. It is possible to understand the last phrase, "against such things there is no law," in the sense that the law was never directed against people who bore these fruit.

5:24. Paul summarized his teachings in this verse. Earlier in Galatians he had stated, "I have been crucified with Christ" (2:20). Now he wrote that everyone who belongs to Christ has "crucified the flesh with its passions and desires." This statement carries the idea that believers reject the flesh and deny themselves the old ways.

5:25–26. These two verses may serve as an introduction to the ideas Paul presented in the following chapter rather than the conclusion of the preceding section. In either case, the truth remains that Paul stated bluntly the necessity of the consistency of believers' actions with the presence of the Holy Spirit in their lives. To put it in the context of what people sometimes say, *You got to walk the talk.* Paul further cautioned his readers not to brag and not to swagger or be arrogant. Such an attitude lacks the humility that represents the fruit of the Spirit. Likewise, arrogant attitudes serve to provoke competition and jealousy.

Focusing on the Meaning

Both sets of my grandparents farmed. Before I started to high school, we moved near one set of them. We also did some farming, mainly growing corn and hay for sale and gardening to raise a lot of our food. So I grew up on or around farms. It was hard and often hot work. I cannot say that I was always a willing farmer. In fact, my hay-hauling, corn-pulling, and gardening as a child and teenager was often done under duress.

Despite my rather grudging participation in our family's farming, I must admit that I felt a great sense of satisfaction when we began to harvest the garden produce or when our hard work paid off in a good harvest. There is truly something amazing and wonderful about seeing the literal *fruit* of labor.

In much the same way, we must work hard to ensure that our lives bear spiritual fruit that will be satisfying to those around us. Our lives should honor our Creator and the Spirit that indwells us by producing love, joy, peace, patience, kindness, and all the other fruit that occurs from walking in the Spirit. Not only will we find great satisfaction ourselves in this kind of life but also we will truly be a blessing to others, and we will be performing an act of worship with our lives. Once we have been set free by God's great grace, we have the freedom to live in such a way that everyone will know we belong to Christ Jesus.

TEACHING PLANS

Teaching Plan—Varied Learning Activities

Connect with Life

1. Greet the members of your class as they arrive, and begin your time together with prayer. Following the prayer, ask the class to think back to the worst neighbor they have ever encountered. Ask each class member to share the things that these people did that made them such difficult neighbors. Record the answers on the board (or poster).

2. After each participant has had an opportunity to share an answer, lead the class to discuss the following questions.

    a. Can you understand why the neighbor acted in a way that was so bothersome?

    b. Was it ever an option to *get even* by being a difficult neighbor in return?

    c. Did you ever *kill your neighbor with kindness* in hope that the neighbor would change?

3. State: *As followers of Christ we should take the high road. Instead of screaming and banging on our rowdy neighbor's door, we might choose to smile and say hello as we pass on the sidewalk. Our neighbors are not only those we live near but also include everyone we meet. As such, we should strive to treat everyone we encounter with love. Today's lesson concerns living by the guidance of God's Spirit. When we act in love, we share the fruit of the Spirit. When we allow ourselves to act in anger or hostility, we give in to the desires of the flesh.*

Guide Bible Study

4. Using the information in the *Study Guide* under the heading "The Sinful Nature (5:16–18)," share with the class an explanation about sins of the flesh and the fruit of the Spirit. Mention that by living in the Spirit, we bear fruit that is not meant for us but to be shared as we love our neighbor.

5. Invite a volunteer from the class to read Galatians 5:13–26. Instruct the class to pay special attention to the desires of the flesh and the fruit of the Spirit.

6. Following the Scripture reading, divide the class into small groups (no more than six people each). Have each group select a timekeeper and a scribe. Give each group a copy of an article (found in a newspaper or magazine, or on the internet) about a person acting out of his or her sinful nature (a list of these acts are found in the *Study Guide* under the heading "Acts of the Sinful Nature"). Inform the groups that they will have twelve minutes to read and then write a synopsis of the story in such a way that the subject of the story will choose to act in accord with the Spirit and not the flesh.

7. When time is up, have each group read the synopsis they wrote containing an alternate ending for the article. When all the groups have shared their synopsis with the class, begin a dialogue about the article using these questions:

   a. How likely do you think the rewritten versions of this article sound like realistic alternatives to the actual story?

   b. Can you understand why the subject of the article decided to act of the flesh and not of the Spirit?

   c. Could you envision yourself making the same decision as the person in the article?

8. Lead the group to suggest words that contrast the kind of life characterized by "the deeds of the flesh" (5:19–21) to the kind of life characterized by "the fruit of the Spirit" (5:22–23). (negative versus positive; destructive versus constructive)

Encourage Application

9. State: *Paul said that by acting of the Spirit, Christians are called to a "higher standard of living," as the Study Guide states. The Jewish laws of the past cannot fulfill this higher standard. Christians can live up to this higher standard by living out the commandment, "Love your neighbor as yourself."*

10. Make sure that each member of the class has a pen or pencil and a piece of paper. Share with the class that you are going to ask them several questions. Ask them to record their answers, not for sharing, but for personal reflection.

    a. What have you done to fulfill the commandment to "love your neighbor as yourself" in the past week?

    b. What is an example, from this past week, when you did *not* "love your neighbor as yourself"?

    c. In the upcoming week what will you do to "love your neighbor as yourself"?

11. End the class in prayer. Ask for the wisdom and strength to "love your neighbor as yourself," showing in our lives the "fruit of the Spirit."

Teaching Plan—Lecture and Questions

Connect with Life

1. Welcome participants as they arrive. Open your time together with prayer. Before the class begins, make two lists on the board (or poster). One list should contain examples of the desires of the flesh. (Examples can be found in the *Study Guide* under the heading "Acts of the Sinful Nature.") The second list should contain examples of the fruit of the Spirit. State: *Imagine someone is writing a book about the class. If the writer was choosing a word from one of these lists to describe you, which list would you like it to be from?* Point out that most people would want the title of their chapter to be from the fruit of the Spirit list.

2. Explain to the class that this Scripture concerns living not by the law but by the Spirit. State that by living a Spirit-led life and avoiding acts of the sinful nature, we share the fruit of the Spirit with the world.

Guide Bible Study

3. Draw the class's attention to an outline of this lesson that you have posted before class began, as follows:

(1) Freedom and Love (Gal. 5:13–15)

(2) The Sinful Nature (Gal. 5:16–18)

(3) Acts of the Sinful Nature (Gal. 5:19–21)

(4) Acts of the Spirit (Gal. 5:22–26)

4. Invite a volunteer to read Galatians 5:13–26. Ask the class to pay attention to what the passage says concerning the sins of the flesh and the fruit of the Spirit.

5. Using information from the *Study Guide* and "Bible Comments" in this *Teaching Guide*, explain briefly the first point of the outline. Then engage the class in a discussion using the following questions:
   - Paul told the Galatian Christians they were "called to be free" (Gal. 5:13, NIV). What might have been his thinking to later say in the same verse that they were to "serve one another"?
   - The whole law is summed up with the commandment, "Love your neighbor as yourself." Why might this have been so objectionable to those who were calling the Galatians to live by the law?

6. Bring the attention of the class back to the posted outline. Explain the second and third outline points by using the information in the *Study Guide* and "Bible Comments" in this *Teaching Guide*.

7. Lead the class to discuss questions 4–6 from the *Study Guide*.

Encourage Application

8. Focus the attention of the class on the fourth outline point. Using the information in the *Study Guide*, explain Galatians 5:22–26. Then lead the class to answer the following questions, keeping their congregation in mind:
   a. Do you think that as a congregation we are showing our neighbors the fruit of the Spirit?
   b. Desires of the flesh are inevitable. How do you see our congregation giving in to these desires?
   c. Do you believe our congregation has any rules that sometimes seem more important than simply loving our neighbor?

9. Refer to the small article "The Fruit of the Spirit" in the *Study Guide*, and lead the class to respond to each question.

10. Close your time together in prayer, asking God to help the class share God's love with the world, beginning in your class, your church, and your community.

NOTES

1. Herman N. Ridderbos, *The Epistle of Paul to the Churches of Galatia* (Grand Rapids, MI: Wm. B. Eerdmans Publishing Co., 1953, 1981 reprint), 200–201.

FOCAL TEXT
Galatians 6:1–10, 14–16

BACKGROUND
Galatians 6

MAIN IDEA
Positive church life includes offering help even to members who have sinned, humbly examining one's own life, supporting church leaders, never giving up in doing good, and continually focusing on Christ.

QUESTION TO EXPLORE
What's life like in a truly good church?

TEACHING AIM
To lead the class to evaluate their church in light of Paul's teachings on how the church was to conduct itself and decide on at least one action they will take in light of this evaluation

LESSON EIGHT
Life in a Good Church

UNIT TWO
The Gospel in Life

BIBLE COMMENTS

Understanding the Context

Because of the power of Paul's writings and the historical influence they have had, it is sometimes easy to forget that first and foremost, Paul ministered as an evangelist, church planter, and pastor. He wrote his letters to deal with issues local congregations faced regularly. As noted in earlier lessons, Galatians dealt specifically with issues related to problems caused by Judaizing Christians. However, as these lessons have demonstrated, the same types of problems have recurred through the ages. Paul's encouragement and message to the Galatians can be applied in today's churches.

At the same time Paul was dealing with specific issues of his day, he was also providing words of challenge and blessing more general in nature. Such was the case in his concluding words to the Galatian believers. In this final section of Galatians, Paul set forth timeless principles that describe what life should be like in a church that honors God.

Interpreting the Scriptures

Carrying and Caring (6:1–6)

6:1. This sentence is the first in a series of exhortations Paul addressed to life within the church. "Caught in any trespass" can be translated as *surprised in any sin*. It most likely meant that the person has been trapped by sin, not caught by others. This understanding fits more directly with what Paul said in the remainder of the sentence. He taught those "who are spiritual" how to respond to those who might be caught in a moral failing. Those who walk in the Spirit are those who bear the fruit of the Spirit. Their response, Paul said, should reflect the fruit of the Spirit by utilizing a "spirit of gentleness," which is indeed one of the elements of the fruit itself. The point of the response is found in the word "restore." The role of the more spiritually mature was more to restore than to reprimand. Paul also stated that those who are involved in the restoration need to be careful lest they allow themselves to fall to similar temptation. One implication is that humility, one aspect of the fruit of the Spirit, should be a part of this restoration. After all, each believer should examine himself or herself during the exercise of this restoration to ensure that he or she does not sin in similar fashion.

6:2. This verse is one of the most quoted passages of Paul's writings. In this second exhortation, Paul commanded Christians to share the burdens they carry. "Burdens" can be translated *oppressive burdens*. By writing this, Paul emphasized one of the crucial differences of life in Christ. Believers become part of a community in which no one operates alone or in a vacuum. The words, "one another's," are emphatic. Because of the connection of this verse to verse 1, "burdens" could mean the oppressive burden of temptation. It more likely means *burdens of any kind*. By bearing "one another's burdens" the law of love referred to in earlier passages will be fulfilled.

6:3–4. The focus of these verses is modesty. Paul intended that his readers understand clearly that foolish or false pride stands in contrast to humility. *Self-inflation is also self-deceit.* In the original language, these words carry more force than they do in English. Paul was not saying that human beings are worthless, but when measured against the divine standard, they are not perfect. Essentially Paul said that believers should not measure themselves against other people. Ultimately, any human glorying must be done in God.

6:5. This statement has become a proverb. It seems to contradict what Paul had just said, but does not. The sense of the wording is that every person is responsible for his or her own behavior before God. "Load" (*burden*) differs from its meaning in verse 2. Here it means the regular day-to-day issues and concerns every person must deal with in life.

6:6. This verse is difficult to place in context. Perhaps Paul intended it to serve as a continuation of what he had been addressing in terms of caring for others, carrying the burdens, and fulfilling the daily responsibilities of life. Or perhaps he intended that it be connected with the warnings he gave in the following verses. Quite likely, Paul simply intended it to be a transitional statement.

Sowing and Blessing (6:7–10)

6:7–8. These verses return to the agricultural imagery Paul used in 5:22–23. Paul may have returned to this theme in what he had just written in the preceding verse about sharing good things. In *Cotton Patch Gospel*, New Testament scholar Clarence Jordan translated the first part of these verses this way, "Don't let anyone pull the wool over your eyes—you can't turn up your nose at God."[1] The word Paul used for "deceived" was widely utilized in the New Testament. It can be translated in a passive fashion, *don't be led astray*. Another way of translating the latter part of that first sentence is, *you can't fool God*. Thus, that which people sow—the good fruit of the Spirit or the deeds of the flesh to which Paul referred in chapter 5—will have returns similar to what was sowed. Paul said that if the deeds of the flesh or corruption are sown, then corruption will be harvested. The corruption he wrote of here can mean physical corruption but can also mean moral decay. A believer's life should yield the fruit of the Spirit. Such a harvest results in the harvest of eternal life.

6:9–10. Even though Paul repeatedly stressed that salvation cannot be earned but must be accepted as a gift, he continually emphasized the need for believers to do good. Christians should constantly seek to be a blessing to others. However, Paul also warned of a danger, that of losing "heart." The image Paul used can mean *become limp* or *grow weary*. One commentator states, "As describing a disheartened farmer the picture is very graphic; as describing the disheartened Galatians, who have found so much previous 'effort' vain, it is equally striking."[2] Paul implored them not to become discouraged but to keep on doing good, especially to and for fellow believers.

Glory in Crucifixion (6:14–16)

In the verses immediately preceding these (6:11–13), Paul reminded his readers of the main theme of Galatians, renouncing the claims of the Judaizers. He returned to that topic here. Believers, Paul said, should not glory in anything they might do and cited his own experience as an example. The only thing in which he would boast, Paul reminded them, was the cross of Christ. He would not boast in his own circumcision or any other qualification. All that, he said, had been crucified with Christ. He was now the new creation of which he had written earlier (2:20). He concluded this statement by embracing anyone who would follow that simple "rule" and providing a very Pauline blessing "upon them, and upon the Israel of God." There are several ways this final phrase might be interpreted. I understand it to mean that Christian Jews and Christian Gentiles are all part of this new creation in Christ.

Focusing on the Meaning

Paul encouraged the Galatians to keep offering help to members who had sinned, humbly examining their own lives, supporting church leaders, never giving up in doing good, and continually focusing on Christ. Those who had the Holy Spirit resident in their lives would do this. It is not easy to bear one's own burdens, to help others bear their burdens, and to keep doing good, all while keeping our "eyes fixed upon Jesus, the author and perfecter of our faith" (Hebrews 12:2). However, if we can do this, life in Christ's church will be what God intended when God created the church. When we live life in the church as God intended, Christ's cross will be glorified, lives will be changed, and the world will become a little better place.

Several years ago, I wrote a free-verse poem that illustrates the principle of Galatians 6:2. I recently revised it in honor of a friend. I think it illustrates what believers should be to one another in the church's life. If we can do this consistently then we can experience life in a truly good church.

WEIGHT LIFTING
Galatians 6:2

It happened suddenly
Before
I
knew it
My
load became too heavy.

So heavy
I
Staggered beneath its weight.
Each successive step on the
    journey
I seemed

to stumble with more and more
efficiency.

It seemed obvious that
soon
I would fall
flat on
My
face.

Crushed beneath
a burden
My
life wasted.
My
heart broken.

So
in terminal desperation
I
cried out for help
from God.

My
voice muffled
by strain of hardship
Now bending
My
back,

Squeezing precious breath from
My
exhausted lungs,
Limited resolve from
My
feeble spirit.

God seemed
not to hear.
Tears rolled down
My
cheeks,
from the pain of the load
from the pain of a desertion
beyond
My
comprehension.

Clumsily
I
cried out again.
Shifted ponderous burden.
God still did not come.

Then I saw
You.
Standing
beside me
With an almost helpless smile.

You
placed
Your
arm around me
Shifted some weight to
Your
own shoulders
not a heavy part but enough for
Me to know
I wasn't alone.

The load no lighter really.
Yet, somehow more bearable

Because
You
were there.

Steps somewhat more certain
Because they were matched by
Yours.
More certain because I noticed
You carried
Your own load too.

Still a bit troubled though
Why had Christ not rushed to
my side? Did he ignore
my agonized plea?
Frustrated still, and a bit
  uncertain.

I turned and saw
You
again
Your
load and some of my load
shared upon
Your
shoulders.

The glass became clearer
for when our eyes met
I saw not
Your
face
but the face of Christ.[3]

TEACHING PLANS

Teaching Plan—Varied Learning Activities

Connect with Life

1. Greet the members of your class as they arrive. Begin the session with a prayer. Ask the class whether they or someone they know have ever done something that made them feel cut off from a group of people they cared about (such as friends, family, teammates, co-workers, etc.) only to later reconcile. Invite anyone who is willing to share about this experience. If no one chooses to respond, encourage the group simply to recall such an occasion.

2. State: *This Scripture passage is centered on the question of what life looks like in a healthy church. Being a healthy congregation includes loving and welcoming people who may have done things in their lives*

many may think would make them unfit to be a part of a Christian church. The passage also points to several other important elements of being a healthy congregation.

Guide Bible Study

3. Divide the class into several small groups, with two to six people in each. Instruct each group to select a scribe and a timekeeper. Provide the following group assignments. (A copy is available in "Teaching Resource Items" for this study at www.baptistwaypress.org. The assignments could also be used as a worksheet with the class as a whole.) When time has expired, the groups will share their answers with the class. As the groups report, write their assigned topics and Scripture verses on the board or a poster, leaving room for writing (see step 4). As reports are given, add insights from the *Study Guide* and from "Bible Comments" in this *Teaching Guide* as seems helpful.

"Share the Burdens" (Galatians 6:1–5)

a. Why did Paul think sharing "burdens" within a Christian community was important?

b. Looking at our own congregation, how do you see burdens being shared?

c. Can a congregation truly be healthy without sharing burdens? Is our congregation healthy? If not, what would you suggest we do to make it healthy?

"Carry Your Load While You Share the Burdens" (Galatians 6:5)

a. Why did Paul think carrying our own "load" while sharing the burdens within a Christian community was important?

b. Looking at our own congregation, how do you see this instruction being fulfilled?

c. Can a congregation truly be healthy without fulfilling this instruction? Is our congregation healthy? If not, what would you suggest we do to make it healthy?

"Share the Resources" (Galatians 6:6)

a. Why did Paul think sharing financial resources to support people who served the Christian community was important?

b. Looking at our own congregation, how do you see this instruction being fulfilled?

c. Can a congregation truly be healthy without sharing in this manner? Is our congregation healthy? If not, what would you suggest we do to make it healthy?

"Share the Harvest" (Galatians 6:7–10)

a. Why did Paul think working together within a Christian community to share the harvest was important?

b. Looking at our own congregation, how do you see our sharing in "the harvest"?

c. Can a congregation truly be healthy without sharing in "the harvest"? Is our congregation healthy? If not, what would you suggest we do to make it healthy?

"Share the Gospel" (Galatians 6:14–16)

a. Why did Paul think emphasizing the gospel within a Christian community was important?

b. Looking at our own congregation, to what extent is the gospel our emphasis?

c. Can a congregation truly be healthy without emphasizing the gospel? Is our congregation healthy? If not, what would you suggest we do to make it healthy?

Encourage Application

4. Refer to each topic on the board or the posters (see step 3). Lead the group to identify at least one action they can take to help their church in this area.

5. Bring the class's attention to a cross you have placed in the front of the room. Enlist someone to read Galatians 6:14–16 again. Point

out the importance of the cross in these verses and in Paul's life. Lead the class to decide on at least one action they will take as individuals or as a class in light of this focus on the cross of Christ. Close with prayer for persistence and willingness in sharing ourselves with one another as a church in light of what Christ has done for us.

Teaching Plan—Lecture and Questions

Connect with Life

1. Draw the class's attention to the small article "Reaping and Sowing" in the *Study Guide*. Either summarize it or give the class several minutes to read it. Then lead the class to discuss it with the questions in the article and with these additional questions:

    a. How do we know whether we are sowing the right types of seeds in our lives?

    b. If someone is an inexperienced "farmer" (a new Christian), should he or she expect to have a smaller crop than an experienced "farmer"? Why or why not?

    c. The article mentions the resources of "fertilizer, sunshine, water, good soil, and a lot of hard work" as being needed to have a good crop. What resources are needed for a good spiritual crop in our lives and in the lives of others? What about in a church? What resources are needed to produce a good church?

2. Inform the class that today we will be seeking to understand what life is like in a truly good church. Point out that the principle of reaping and sowing applies to life in the church, too.

Guide Bible Study

3. Draw the attention of the class to an outline for the study that you have posted, as follows:

Life in a Good Church
(Galatians 6:1–10, 14–16)

Share the Burdens (6:1:5)

Carry Your Load While You Share the Burdens (6:5)

Share the Resources (6:6)

Share the Harvest (6:7–10)

Share the Gospel (6:14–16)

---

4. On the board (or poster) make two columns titled "Healthy Church" and "Unhealthy Church." Ask the class to name characteristics that make a church, or a congregation, either healthy or unhealthy, in their opinion. List the answers in the appropriate column.

5. Encourage the class to follow in their Bibles as you (or someone you have enlisted) read Galatians 6:1–10, 14–16. Have the class keep in mind the two lists that they just created while listening to the Scripture being read.

6. Following the reading of the Scripture, use the outline points and information from the *Study Guide* to explain and apply the verses, adding information from "Bible Comments" in this *Teaching Guide.* Use these discussion questions at the appropriate points in the outline, too:

    a. Galatians 6:1 speaks of restoring "in a spirit of gentleness" members "caught in any trespass." Is there anything like this on our "Healthy Church" list? Why not? What would this look like within our congregation?

    b. Galatians 6:2 says we are to "Bear one another's burdens, and thereby fulfill the law of Christ." How can we carry someone else's burdens? What is the law of Christ that it would fulfill?

    c. Galatians 6:2 and 6:5 seem to be giving different messages. What do you think these verses are saying?

    d. Verse 10 speaks of working for the good of all and especially for the family of believers. As a congregation, do you think we are as supportive of one another as we need to be?

Encourage Application

7. Lead the class to answer the questions in the *Study Guide.*

8. Refer to and lead the class to review each of the points in "Life in a Good Church Involves Sharing" in the *Study Guide.*

9. Refer to each of the outline points in step 3 and ask, *How well do you think our church does this?* Then ask of each outline point, *What actions do you think we need to take to help our church become a "good church" in this area? Which are we willing to do?*

10. Close in prayer that the class will be willing to take action that will strengthen your congregation and show Christ to the world.

NOTES

1. Clarence Jordan, *Cotton Patch Gospel: Paul's Epistles* (Macon, GA: Smyth & Helwys, 2004), 101. Clarence Jordan, who died in 1969, was a New Testament scholar and Christian ethicist. A Baptist, he is best known for the establishment of Koinonia Farms (near Americus, Georgia) and for his influence on Millard and Linda Fuller, founders of Habitat for Humanity.

2. R. Alan Cole, *Galatians*, Tyndale New Testament Commentaries, vol. 9 (Leicester, England and Grand Rapids, MI: Inter-Varsity Press and Wm. B. Eerdmans, Publishing Co., 2nd ed., 1989), 230.

3. "Weight Lifting: Galatians 6:2," Copyright 1993, Michael E. (Mike) Williams, Sr. Used by permission of Michael E. (Mike) Williams, Sr. Originally published in Pamela Rosewell Moore, *When Spring Comes Late: Finding Your Way through Depression* (Grand Rapids: Chosen Books, 2000). Revised for a friend, Deemie Naugle, on the occasion of her twenty-fifth anniversary at Dallas Baptist University, November 4, 2008.

FOCAL TEXT
1 Thessalonians 1

BACKGROUND
1 Thessalonians 1;
2:13–14, 19–20; 3:6–9;
2 Thessalonians 1:1–4

MAIN IDEA
Thank God for a church
that is an example in
faith, hope, and love.

QUESTION TO EXPLORE
For what about your church
do you thank God?

TEACHING AIM
To lead the class to identify
qualities of a church for
which to thank God and
to express thanks to God
as they identify positive
qualities in their church

LESSON NINE
Thank God for Such a Church!

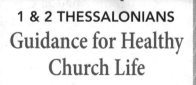

1 & 2 THESSALONIANS
Guidance for Healthy Church Life

BIBLE COMMENTS

Understanding the Context

The special relationship between Paul and the Thessalonian believers is easily seen when reading 1 and 2 Thessalonians. Paul's affection for the church at Thessalonica stemmed in part from his initial preaching of the gospel to them and his founding of the community. The Acts of the Apostles briefly notes Paul's time in the city (Acts 17:1–9). The Acts account may indicate Paul spent only a short period of time in the city before he and Silas were forced to leave and travel by night to Beroea (Acts 17:10). While the account in Acts and the accounts in the Thessalonian letters can be difficult to reconcile, one point of connection seems likely: Acts indicates the infant community at Thessalonica was composed of "a great many of the devout Greeks and not a few of the leading women" (Acts 17:4).[1] First Thessalonians indicates that the readers or listeners would mainly be composed of Gentiles.

With affectionate concern for the new and untried believers in Thessalonica, Paul was anxious about their welfare as he indicated in 1 Thessalonians 3:1–5. Perhaps based on his own observations and experiences, he was concerned that this group would experience afflictions that might cause some to falter in the faith. For this reason, and since Paul was unable to journey personally to Thessalonica, he sent his envoy Timothy. When Timothy returned, Paul was overjoyed to learn that the Thessalonians remained steadfast in the faith (1 Thessalonians 3:6).

Paul's anxiety for the newly-formed Christian church in Thessalonica was probably well-founded. The city presented opportunities for new Christians to be drawn back into paganism. Thessalonica was one of the largest cities in the Roman province of Macedonia and was strategically located on the major east-west road called the Via Egnatia and also at the head of the Thermaic Gulf. Both opportunity and challenge abounded in this city. Opportunity existed to share the gospel with the diverse Greco-Roman population comprising the city and with traders and pilgrims passing through it. Challenges existed, for it was a city steeped in the worship traditions of the various gods and goddesses of the first century.

Since Paul was unable to travel to Thessalonica, he utilized the form of letter writing to continue his connection with and instruction to this infant Christian community. First Thessalonians probably represents the earliest preserved Christian writing. Written around AD 49–50, it represents a revolutionary approach for connectivity with churches spread over a diverse geographical region. Paul used and modified the typical Greco-Roman letter writing style into an enduring tradition of Christian letter writing. As with most letters in the ancient world, one person would read and others would listen.

Interpreting the Scriptures

Greetings to a Thriving Church (1:1)

1:1. First words make a lasting impression. Paul's first words of greeting, while brief, tell us much about him, the community of believers at Thessalonica, and his theological outlook. First, Paul did not write his letter by himself alone: he networked with others, specifically his coworkers, Silvanus and Timothy. Paul was not a *lone ranger* in missions; rather he understood the importance of cooperation and partnership in spreading the gospel.

Second, Paul did not pull out his apostolic calling card of authority. Paul was simply Paul. His unadorned and simple introduction allows one to realize, even before the main body of this letter, that a bond of affection, mutual respect, and love existed between Paul and the believers in Thessalonica. The depth of this love is revealed in his coming thanksgiving for them.

Paul also created a signature Christian greeting: grace and peace. Paul combined the typical Jewish greeting of "peace" (*shalom*) with the word "grace" (*charis*), which is a play on the Greek word for greeting. These two characteristics, with "grace" always first in Paul's letters, are reminders that grace always precedes peace in one's life or church.

An Exemplary Church (1:2–5)

1:2–3. Paul began with a thanksgiving section that became typical in later Christian letters. By starting with the words, "we give thanks," this thanksgiving section began on a positive note for Paul's listeners. With initial praise, listeners were more receptive to any later advice or admonitions. Also, Paul was never shy about heaping praise on those who demonstrated the Christlike walk of life. His effusive thanksgiving was specifically directed towards three characteristics of the Thessalonians: faith, love, and hope. Paul utilized this triad of Christian virtues in later letters to other churches (1 Corinthians 13:13; Romans 5:1–5; and Ephesians 4:2–5). Paul, interestingly, qualified each of these three characteristics in these verses.

Paul began by describing the Thessalonians' faith as a "work of faith" (1 Thess. 1:3). Work and faith are not terms often associated together in Pauline thought, but Paul believed faith generated deeds. Good actions can originate from many sources, but for Christians, faith provides the energy and creativity to act on behalf of another in God's name. Paul may also imply that at times faith is a gut-wrenching struggle. One is reminded of the man who pleaded to Jesus for healing for his son and cried out, "I believe; help my unbelief" (Mark 9:24).

Paul commended the Thessalonians for their love, but not love as an emotion or a *feel-good* experience. He praised them for their "labor of love." Too often love is sentimentalized and romanticized. For contemporary society, one falls into or out of love with ease. Paul, however, understood love as an act of the will. He was grateful for a community of believers that labored, not in self gratification, but in love for one another.

"Steadfastness of hope" implies that the Thessalonians had persevered in the face of difficult situations. While the particular situations are not clearly stated (1 Thess. 2:14), the bedrock for the Thessalonians' assurance is clear: trust in Jesus Christ. Hope placed in Christ, as the Thessalonians' lives illustrated, endures with the expectation of God's faithfulness in all our experiences.

1:4. With great feeling and affection, Paul bestowed on his listeners the title of "beloved by God." No greater epithet could Paul write over the Thessalonians to illustrate his thankfulness for who they were. And no greater assurance could the Thessalonians cling to in difficult times. Paul also declared they were chosen by God: they were elect. This point carries a profound theological import, calling to mind the long Hebrew Scripture tradition of God's selection and choices of individuals and groups through history. To be chosen brings both grace and obligation. The Thessalonians had experienced grace, and Paul was grateful that their lives were witness to fulfilling the obligations of being chosen.

1:5. How did Paul know the Thessalonians were chosen? It was simple; he witnessed in their lives the marks of their acceptance of the gospel in faith, love, and hope. The term "gospel" meant the life, death, resurrection, and saving significance of Jesus. It was a message proclaimed in human words, but, as Paul noted, he delivered it in power through the Holy Spirit. Paul was utterly convinced of its truth and bet his life on it. The Thessalonians, no doubt, were inspired by a messenger such as Paul who proclaimed truth with such clarity and conviction.

Imitation and Inspiration (1:6–10)

1:6. The earliest Christian believers did not have handbooks outlining how to live a new life in Christ. Instead they learned by observation. Paul told them to turn their gaze on him, his coworkers, and Jesus. These lives were their model. On the surface, this claim gives an audacious arrogance to Paul. Who was Paul to consider himself a model to follow? Yet contained in Paul's words is a sense of joyous burden that is tempered by humility. Even a brief sampling of his life illustrates how he learned by imitating Jesus' own way of the cross (1 Cor. 11:23–27).

1:7-8. By imitating others, the Thessalonians themselves became a community of inspiration and an example for others, even in spite of persecution and distress. Their example even spread beyond the local city of Thessalonica into the Roman provinces of Macedonia (in which Thessalonica was located) and also neighboring Achaia (southern Greece). This social network of Christian communication, far from spreading bad news and gossip, spread the good news of early Christians practicing their simple and powerful faith.

Not only did the witness about Thessalonian believers extend into the nearby Roman provinces, but Paul also declared with unsubdued pride, and perhaps a little hyperbole, that the news of their faith in God had spread everywhere. Paul used the phrase "the word of the Lord has sounded forth from you" to describe this spreading witness. While this phrase might mean the Thessalonians sent out their own missionaries, most likely it means that their local example of faithfulness was being voiced by others who passed the inspirational story of the Thessalonians onto whoever would listen.

1:9. Paul acknowledged the reasons for the spread of the Thessalonians' story. First, they showed hospitality to him and his coworkers. Hospitality was no small feat in the ancient world. It reveals the depth of commitment to a way of life and to relationships. This hospitality was even more significant when practiced during times of greatest challenge, such as economic or social struggles.

Second, the Thessalonians' story spread everywhere because they abandoned idols and turned to God. Such a statement indicates Paul's ministry focus was with Gentile converts. To join this new movement announced by Paul was a radical experience for the Thessalonians. It meant leaving behind familiar local deities and comfortable cultic rituals. A transformed and radically new lifestyle made old neighbors and acquaintances suspicious of this group of believers.

For Paul, however, the story of the Thessalonians' conversion was special not only for rejecting a way of life, that is, worship of idols, but also by picking up a way of life, serving God. In Paul's understanding, service to God was demonstrated in service to the community through works of faith and labors of love.

1:10. At the heart of Paul's theology was a belief that the resurrection of Jesus marked the beginning of a new age and that the return of Jesus signaled the conclusion of the old age. The new age has come but not fully. The old age continues, but it is passing away. We live in an already-but-not-yet time. This belief guided Paul's mission work and ethical outlook on life. He rejoiced that the Thessalonians also anticipated God's "Son from heaven." He understood their lives of faith, love, and hope as examples of what it meant to live in this in-between time.

Focusing on the Meaning

Paul's first words to the Thessalonians declared his thanksgiving for their characteristics of faith, love, and hope. These qualities, along with imitation of Christ, demonstrated their faithfulness. Paul illustrated that encouragement and praise are not options or luxury but a way to consistently support one other. Like rooting for a marathon runner at mile eighteen of a twenty-six mile race, authentic praise and thanksgiving undergird a person's spirit and encourages the person on the Christian journey.

Paul's letter is a reminder for us to consider the various qualities and spiritual virtues that make a church. Every church is unique and has its own particular characteristics. We should look within our own communities of faith and search for those positive qualities that honor Christ, and, when found, celebrate with a word of thanksgiving, both publicly and privately.

The characteristics Paul praised within the Thessalonian church—faith, love, and hope—represent the apex of Christian virtues that are found in healthy and thriving churches. Communities of love and faith are not created overnight but require work and labor. Paul's words challenge us to remember that building the community of faith may not be an easy task, but the foundations, walls, and roof of the church will always be sustained by the faith and love freely given among its members. Of course, hope, in the face of and in spite of circumstances, continues to renew the spirit of all within the church.

When believers experience the positive qualities of being the church and affirm one another, the witness is carried beyond the church's walls. Just as a country is recognized by its flag, so is a church recognized by its positive (or negative) qualities. If energy, enthusiasm, and love are found in the church, these characteristics will tumble out to the larger community. When this witness happens, then the words of Paul take on special meaning: "your faith in God has become known, so that we have no need to speak about it" (1 Thess. 1:8).

TEACHING PLANS

Teaching Plan—Varied Learning Activities

Connect with Life

1. Lead the group to think about Thanksgiving and to call out the things they customarily do for this holiday (for example, eat a big dinner, watch football, plan for after-Thanksgiving sales, etc.). Ask, *How much time do you—or most people—actually spend giving thanks?* Or, *In what ways do you express thanks?* Allow for spoken answers, if any. Then ask, *When you do give thanks, at Thanksgiving or any other time, do you normally express thanks for your church?*

2. Say, *As we start this study on 1 and 2 Thessalonians, we'll look at Paul's words of thanks for the little church in Thessalonica and think about how his message applies to our church.*

Guide Bible Study

3. Invite someone to read 1 Thessalonians 1:1–2. On a classroom map or on maps printed in participants' Bibles, locate Thessalonica. Refer to and present information about Thessalonica from paragraph two of the lesson in the *Study Guide*. Be sure to note that it was a major center of business and culture and was highly cosmopolitan, having a rich mixture of people from various ethnic, social, and religious backgrounds. Lead the group to discuss how this bustling city of the first century is like and unlike your city today.

   Enlist someone to read Acts 17:1–14. Ask, *What can we conclude about Paul's experience in preaching the gospel in Thessalonica? Would you say he was successful? Why?*

   Ask, *Based on these verses in Acts and what we know about Thessalonica in that day, what could you conclude about the earliest group of Christian believers in that city? What would have been their religious or social background? What problems or obstacles would they have faced?* In addition, lead the group to identify similarities and differences with that early church and your church today.

Also ask, *Have any of you ever tried to start a small group or organization from scratch? What kinds of challenges or problems did you encounter? What might have been challenges for the tiny group of brand-new Christians at Thessalonica as they attempted to craft a church?* (Some suggestions might be: communication with one another and the larger Christian community; qualifications for membership and for leadership; logistics such as meeting times and places; figuring out what to do when they came together, etc.)

4. Lead the group to read 1 Thessalonians 1:2–3 in as many translations as are available. (You may want to locate and bring a few extra translations of these verses.) Ask the class to imagine or brainstorm what Paul might have had in mind with the phrases in verse 3: "your work produced by faith, your labor prompted by love, and your endurance inspired by hope" (NIV). Encourage them to consider your church and their own lives as they respond.

5. Ask, *How do you think Paul heard about what was going on in the Thessalonian church? Do you think he heard more good news or more bad news about them?*

   Divide into three groups. (If more than eighteen people are present, provide duplicate assignments so groups will not be larger than six people each.) Each group is to prepare a news account of the establishment and growth of the church based on 1 Thessalonians 1:4–10. The account should cover as much information as possible that is included in the biblical text. Group one should write it for a traditional daily newspaper. Group two should write it for a traditional television news report (providing *just the facts*, for example). Group three should write the report for an edgy television news show or web site (presenting the information in an excited manner, for example). Allow several minutes for the exercise, and then call for performances. (A copy of these instructions is available in "Teaching Resource Items" for this study at www.baptistwaypress.org.)

   Be sure each group covers points such as these: loved by God; chosen by God; the gospel came with word, power, the Holy Spirit, and conviction; the people followed Paul and his example; the Thessalonians also became examples who were well-known among other Christian communities.

Encourage Application

6. State that this passage is Paul's letter of commendation to the Thessalonian church. Divide into small groups of three to six people each. Hand out paper and pen to each group. If you like, you can hand out a pretty note card. Ask each group to think of things about their church for which to thank God and then to write a note of commendation to your church. If time permits, read some of the notes aloud. Lead the groups to consider forwarding the notes to the pastor or other leaders.

    Conclude with a prayer of thanksgiving for your church and its ministries.

Teaching Plan—Lecture and Questions

Connect with Life

1. Ask, *When is the last time you wrote a thank-you note?* You could also ask further questions about whether the notes were handwritten, typed, or e-mailed. Invite the group to tell about the last time they did so. Also ask, *For what things do people normally write thank-you notes?*

2. Suggest that this passage expresses Paul's thanks to God for the church in Thessalonica. Encourage the group to look for why he was thankful.

Guide Bible Study

3. Enlist someone to read Acts 17:1–9. Refer to and present information about Thessalonica from paragraph two of the lesson in the *Study Guide.* Include information also on the ethnic, social, and religious background of the earliest Christian church there.

    Also explain that 1 and 2 Thessalonians may well have been the earliest books of the New Testament, written about A.D. 49. The two letters are Paul's pastoral instructions for the new church in Thessalonica and guidance for the questions and struggles they faced. (See under the heading "1 and 2 Thessalonians in the New Testament" in "Introducing 1 and 2 Thessalonians" in the *Study Guide.*

4. Invite someone to read 1 Thessalonians 1:1–3. Emphasize the "work produced by faith," "labor prompted by love," and "endurance inspired by hope" in verse 3 (NIV). Lead the group to think of examples in your church of each of these. Then ask for examples in their personal spiritual lives, or of other people they know well, that illustrate any of these.

5. Explain that in 1 Thessalonians 1:4–10, Paul recounted the spiritual history of the church in Thessalonica. Call for someone to read the verses, and invite the group to note or underline phrases that describe the progress of the growth of the church. You may want to write these on the markerboard. Some of the points to note include these: *loved by God; chosen by God; the gospel came with word, power, the Holy Spirit, and conviction; the people followed Paul and his example; the Thessalonians also became models and well-known among other Christian communities.* Ask, *Which of these descriptions could be applied to our church's history? Which could be applied to our own spiritual lives?* Also ask, *Is it appropriate or meaningful to compare the Thessalonian church with our church or ourselves? Why or why not?*

Encourage Application

6. Refer to questions 2, 3, and 4 at the end of the lesson in the *Study Guide.* Lead the group to work through them. Then refer to the Question to Explore, "For what about your church do you thank God?" Encourage responses. Challenge people to pray for their church, thanking God for it.

NOTES ——————————————————————————————————

1. Unless otherwise indicated, all Scripture translations in lessons 9–13 are from the New Revised Standard Version Bible.

FOCAL TEXT
1 Thessalonians 2:1–12

BACKGROUND
1 Thessalonians 2:1–12; 5:12–13

MAIN IDEA
The leaders God wants serve God and the church with integrity, gentleness, loving concern, hard work, and persistent faithfulness.

QUESTION TO EXPLORE
What qualities should a church look for in its leaders?

TEACHING AIM
To lead adults to identify qualities of church leaders who are to be affirmed and followed

LESSON TEN
The Leadership God Wants

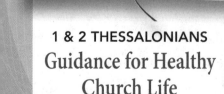

1 & 2 THESSALONIANS
Guidance for Healthy Church Life

BIBLE COMMENTS

Understanding the Context

Paul's great affection and praise for the Thessalonian church runs from 1 Thessalonians 1:2 through 3:13. This lesson's focal verses (2:1–12), while falling within Paul's thanksgiving, have two overarching purposes. One is apologetic, that is, a defense of Paul's ministry while ministering in Thessalonica. The second is more subtle. Paul presented his conduct while in their midst as a leadership model for the Thessalonians to follow.

In Paul's defense of his ministry, he frequently employed sets of negative and positive attributes related to his conduct. He illustrated how his actions in no way hindered the spread of the gospel and how his conduct and words were delivered in a manner beyond reproach. That Paul must make such a defense implies that criticism circulated about his actions and leadership style. This criticism may have stemmed from comparisons made between Paul and others who preached or taught in the cities of Greece.

One of the contexts, therefore, presupposed by 1 Thessalonians is the prevalence of wandering philosophers and teachers traveling throughout the Mediterranean world. In an oral culture, storytelling, new teachings, and lively dramas captured the attention of the crowds in the city. Wandering teachers or philosophers could eke out a living by demonstrating their skills in oratory and by dangling new teachings in the marketplace. Their philosophical teachings attempted to promote particular ethical ways of living.[1] Therefore, much of the same language used by Paul might sound like one of the schools of philosophy represented by the wandering teachers. Sometimes under the guise of teaching, peddlers of this or that philosophy would use their skillful words to reap personal financial benefit. In today's text, a reader frequently will note how Paul sought to distance himself from these peddlers of philosophy.

Paul also laid before the Thessalonians a model to imitate: himself. As last week's lesson emphasized, Christians in the first century had no books or tracts to guide them about living as believers. Paul presented in 1 Thessalonians 2:1–12 a variety of practical *dos* and *don'ts* for how to live a life worthy of God. Paul especially modeled for the

Thessalonians a leadership style based on self-giving and the conviction of God's approval of his ministry.

Interpreting the Scriptures

Leading to Please God (2:1–4)

2:1–2. Paul alluded to his experience in the city of Philippi, which was located approximately ninety-five miles east on the Egnatia road. According to the account in the Acts of the Apostles, Paul and his coworker Silas, because of their preaching of the gospel in Philippi, were beaten, imprisoned, and finally expelled from the city (Acts 16:16–40). No doubt some rumor of their treatment reached Thessalonica.

Paul specifically noted his suffering and shameful treatment at the hands of Philippian officials. In the first-century world, to be dishonored or shamed was one of the worst burdens to bear. Paul's public humiliation was a social stigma, and many in Thessalonica would have regarded him with great suspicion: Would the trouble-maker from Philippi bring trouble also to Thessalonica? Paul, however, with courage in God, brought his message of the good news of Jesus to the Thessalonians. Gratefully, as Paul noted, the message did not fall on deaf ears. Individuals both listened to and accepted it.

2:3. Perhaps rumors circulated about what happened in Philippi or about the content of Paul's teaching that caused the suffering and shame. Slander has speedy feet. For this reason, Paul reminded the Thessalonians that his message did not originate in "deceit," "impure motives," or "trickery." Paul found himself presenting a defense for his ministry leadership against any who challenged his inner motives and his external actions in Thessalonica.

While some translations use the word "deceit" in this verse, a better description is *error.* Paul understood his message as built on a foundation of truth without error. Likewise his message was grounded in self-giving and humility. Finally Paul emphasized his work was not based on dishonest methods. His approach to sharing the gospel was consistent with openness and integrity. The triad of corrupt motives, that is, deceit, impurity, and trickery, represented standard charges brought against false prophets and teachers. Paul's missionary activities did not fall into these shady categories.

2:4. What makes people tick? What makes them get up in the morning and gives them energy? Or in Paul's case, what kept him singing in a Philippian jail cell, trudging along a Roman road (always with one eye cast over his shoulder), or spreading his message in Thessalonica? What was the motivation? For Paul the answer and goal was simple: "to please God." This motive was in sharp contrast to pleasing people and accruing the personal benefits of popularity.

Leading with Humility and Compassion (2:5–8)

2:5–6. Paul felt compelled once again to show how his message did not stem from wrong motives. This time he called God as a witness to his actions. Just as in verse 3 where Paul used a series of negatives to illustrate what his motives were not, he once again used negatives. He emphasized that his message did not flatter in order to gain financial reward.

This motive might seem strange, but many wandering philosophers and teachers crowded the streets of cities like Thessalonica. They peddled their own special type of teaching—for a fee. Hucksters, snake-oil sellers, and silver-tongued orators could take advantage of gullible individuals who were willing to part with a couple of coins. Paul, an itinerant Judean moving from place to place, would easily get lumped in with such a con group. In no uncertain terms, however, Paul denied that personal profit was a motivating factor for any of his words.

Paul also denied that he sought praise. As noted in the comments on 2:1–2, honor was a dominant value in the ancient world. The streets, theaters, fountains, and buildings in Thessalonica were testimonies to the power of honor. Patrons built these structures in order to receive praise and glory from the public. To receive public honor was to have the most valuable resource available in the ancient world. Building teachings with elegant and flowing words would give honor as readily as building a theater or fountain of stone. Yet Paul denied that his words were constructed to envelop him in personal honor.

2:7. Paul suggested, however, that making demands, both financial and honor, on the Thessalonians was within his rights as an apostle of

Christ. Paul was reminding the Thessalonians that itinerant apostles were often granted certain privileges when visiting local congregations. In 1 Corinthians 9:3–18 these rights included food, drink, and accompaniment by a spouse.

In sharp contrast to an authority based on demand, Paul used the image of a nurse caring for her children to describe his leadership style among the Thessalonians. Paul often used a variety of images to illustrate his roles within the churches. He did not shy away from applying a feminine characteristic to his ministry. Far from the *take charge and demand* style, Paul conveyed the idea of loving attentiveness that is filled with care and concern. This type of leadership style was characterized by giving rather than demanding.

2:8. Paul summarized his time with the Thessalonians by stating a fact readily known; he shared himself with them. This style of leadership modeled the life of Jesus, the one who gave wholly of himself. The Lord's Supper is a remembrance of the supreme giving of Christ. Each time we take the bread and cup, the body and the blood, the intimacy of giving reveals itself. In like manner, Paul left a part of himself behind at Thessalonica as the Thessalonians feasted on his ministry.

The Goal of Leadership (2:9–12)

2:9. Paul noted that he labored among the Thessalonians in order not to burden them with any financial responsibilities. Paul also resisted reliance on the Thessalonians because he modeled for the believers how the gospel was practiced in everyday work circumstances. Paul did not mention his particular work, but traditionally he is associated with leather work, specifically tent-making (Acts 18:3). No matter what the work, Paul demonstrated persistence in his work, day and night. The ultimate goal of all his labor was the proclamation of the good news.

2:10. On trial for his ministry conduct, Paul called into the docket two witnesses to testify: the Thessalonians themselves and God. Previously Paul listed negative characteristics that he rejected; now he named three positive aspects of conduct that he and his coworkers embraced: "purity," "uprightness," and "blamelessness." This triad of piety illustrated Paul's right standing before God in purity and before the Thessalonians in uprightness. In both Paul's vertical relationship and horizontal relationships, he was blameless.

2:11. In this verse, Paul shifted the image from a nurse with children to a father with children. Paul used one of the most potent cultural values available in the ancient world: kinship. Brothers, sisters, nurse, father— these terms were just a few Paul used to highlight that the new age had come. The lineage ties generated by blood were replaced by the ties that bound the family created by the good news of Jesus Christ.

2:12. Paul used three words to describe the father's actions: "urging," "encouraging," and "pleading." Contained within these words is the important concept of instruction and advice that in the ancient world was called *parenesis*. This instruction or exhortation was typically given by an authority figure and was advice either to stop doing negative actions and/or to start doing positive actions.

The advice issued by Paul to the Thessalonians, and by implication to all believers, was to "lead a life worthy of God." Once again the idea of honor is seen. A life pure, upright, and blameless, as modeled by Paul and his coworkers, was the life Paul set forth as a goal for the Thessalonians. Paul was implying that one's actions reflected on one's group and also on God. In a sense, Paul presented a challenge to the Thessalonians by implying that God's honor was based on how they lived their lives.

Paul ended by acknowledging God as the ultimate source that called the Thessalonians into God's kingdom and glory. This simple description, however, had significant political implications. The language sounded an ominous challenge to the power of the Roman Empire. Only one kingdom or empire and its glory was of preeminence for the first century. To speak a word about another kingdom was a courageous form of leadership for Paul. It was equally a courageous act of rebellion by all who chose to join this new reign under the leadership of God.

Focusing on the Meaning

Every church finds itself at some point in its life deciding on leaders, including pastors, staff, and laity. These times happen frequently. Surveys will be distributed, job descriptions written, and résumés received and read. One of the often unvoiced but ever-present questions is: *Will he or she make a good leader?* At other times, a person on the other side of the equation might ask himself or herself: *Will I make a good leader?*

These few verses from Paul's pen provide a window into the essence of good and effective Christian leadership. Using Paul as a model, one can first describe what leadership is not. Leadership is not about self-aggrandizement. A Pauline-type leader does not seek his or her own way and is not seduced by externals such as praise, money, or public opinion. On the other hand, in a positive vein, leadership is characterized by a God-centered message in which a leader displays both certainty and humility. These two characteristics are not always easily reconciled.

Certainty is that sense of conviction and passion that the goal for which one strives is oriented towards the very heart of God's hope for the world, a hope characterized by justice and right relationships between God and humanity. This leadership characteristic of certainty is balanced by humility. Certainty, especially in misplaced convictions and goals, can lead to arrogance and a spirit of self righteousness. In this approach, one's convictions can justify any means. Humility, however, tempers certainty. Humility is the characteristic that allows relationships to thrive. It was the type of humility Paul demonstrated by way of suffering and of giving of his very self to the Thessalonians.

Perhaps leadership as illustrated by Paul's life is ultimately about loving rather than coercing others into lives worthy of God. Paul acknowledged he had the leadership power to demand, but chose tenderly to care, plead, and encourage. In other words, Paul chose a leadership style of love modeled after Jesus' own life.

TEACHING PLANS

Teaching Plan—Varied Learning Activities

Connect with Life

1. Make copies of the following anagram games and distribute them for the class to solve, either in small groups or individually. (A copy is available in "Teaching Resource Items" for this study at www.baptistwaypress.org.) You could also write them on the markerboard in advance and work as a whole group. Also, you could give the hint that the *Study Guide* is helpful in solving the anagrams, for the anagrams come from the subheads for each section of this lesson. After a few minutes, provide the answers.

   1. GYEINTRIT _ _ _ _ _ _ _ _ _
   2. SLESEGTNEN _ _ _ _ _ _ _ _ _ _
   3. IOVLGN NENCROC _ _ _ _ _ _ _ _ _ _ _ _
   4. RHDA KRWO _ _ _ _ _ _ _ _
   5. STERSIPNET SHENFLAFTHIS

      _ _ _ _ _ _ _ _ _ _ _ _ _ _ _ _ _ _ _
   6. GRNESNPIODN OT LPEIAHDHSER

      _

Answers:

1. Integrity
2. Gentleness
3. Loving Concern
4. Hard Work
5. Persistent Faithfulness
6. Responding to Leadership

State that this lesson focuses on Paul's words to the Thessalonians about the qualities required for effective church leaders. Invite the group to see how the anagrams apply.

Guide Bible Study

2. Divide into small groups, and provide pencil and paper for each group. Assign a group one or more of the solved anagrams from step 1 plus the applicable section in the *Study Guide*. Then, for each of the qualities, the group is to develop a working definition based on clues from the Scripture text. After about five minutes for work, ask groups to write their definitions on a poster or board for display and then read and explain them as needed. The group is to read its assigned Scripture passage as part of its report. (A copy of the assignments is available in "Teaching Resource Items" for this study at www.baptistwaypress.org.) As groups report, provide explanatory comments from the *Study Guide* and "Bible Comments" in this *Teaching Guide*.

Encourage Application

3. Once more, working as a full group or in small groups, invite the class to create an acrostic for the word *leader*. You could write the capital letters in a column on the markerboard, or you could distribute paper and pencil and instruct each group to do so. To construct the acrostic, the group is to choose a word that starts with each letter and that would characterize an effective church leader. For example, for *L* you might choose *loving*; for *E* you might choose empathy, and so on. After completing the exercise, call for each group's report of the acrostic.

4. Invite the class to work through the leadership self-analysis exercise in the small article titled "Leadership" in the *Study Guide*. Or, if your group knows one another well, divide into pairs. Referring to the leadership qualities identified in this study, say, *I want each of you to think of a way you have grown or improved in one of these qualities. Also, focus on one or two of the qualities your partner dem-*

onstrates especially well. Encourage the pairs to affirm one another as they discuss their thoughts.

Teaching Plan—Lecture and Questions

Connect with Life

1. Ask whether anyone has ever served on a search committee for a pastor or other leader in a church. You could also find a guest speaker who has worked on a search committee. Spend a few minutes interviewing the person about his or her experience, focusing on how the person decided what qualities or experience to look for in the candidate and how he or she determined whether a candidate would be appropriate or not.

2. State that Paul wanted the new church in Thessalonica to have good instruction on evaluating leaders.

Guide Bible Study

3. Invite the class to open their *Study Guides* and follow the subheads as you guide conversation on the text. Enlist someone to read each Scripture passage as you lead the group to consider the information under a given subhead. Pause after each section to summarize and answer any questions. As you lead the study, write the subheads on the markerboard: "Integrity"; "Gentleness"; "Loving Concern"; "Hard Work"; "Persistent Faithfulness"; "Responding to Leadership."

4. Either after you have completed this review or as a part of it, lead a discussion with questions such as the following and/or those from the *Study Guide*:

   a. Regarding "Integrity" (2:2–6).

      (1) Is it easy to spot greed in a person or to spot people who are "looking for praise from men"? How?

    (2) Can some people go too far as they try to avoid "looking for praise from men"?

b. Regarding "Gentleness" (2:6–7):

    (1) Who are some people you know or know of (perhaps including literary characters) who are "gentle"? What traits, qualities or actions do you see in these people?

    (2) Is gentleness valued in our society? If so, where and when?

c. Regarding "Loving Concern" (2:8):

    (1) What are some examples you have seen of a church leader showing loving concern?

    (2) Is it possible to be an effective church leader without demonstrating loving concern?

d. Regarding "Hard Work" (2:9):

    (1) What was Paul's work?

    (2) Is it possible to work too hard in the Lord's work?

e. Regarding "Persistent Faithfulness" (2:10–12):

    (1) What does it take to maintain "persistent faithfulness"?

    (2) What examples of "persistent faithfulness" can you think of?

f. Regarding "Responding to Leadership" (5:12–13):

    (1) Should church members always respect any leader, even if he or she does not seem to be working hard or effectively? Why? How should this be done?

    (2) How can church members demonstrate respect and regard for leaders?

g. Additional questions:

    (1) How would a search committee discern any of these qualities in a candidate?

    (2) Are some of these qualities more important than others? Explain.

Encourage Application

5. Review the leadership qualities that are displayed (see step 3). Refer to question 3 in "Questions" in the *Study Guide*. Lead the class to think about your church and its leaders in responding to this question.

6. Close with prayer that your church leaders may be blessed with each of the qualities identified in this text and that as the need arises, God will raise up new leaders with these qualities.

NOTES

1. These philosopher-teachers could be Stoics, Cynics, or Epicureans. Stoics sought freedom from passion and pain. Cynics taught the importance of self-control over one's desires. Epicureans sought to maximize pleasure and minimize pain.

FOCAL TEXT
1 Thessalonians 4:1–12; 5:14–24

BACKGROUND
1 Thessalonians 4:1–12; 5:14–24

MAIN IDEA
Christians are to live so as to both please God and win the respect of other people, especially people outside the church.

QUESTION TO EXPLORE
How can we live distinctively as Christians and at the same time win the respect of people outside the church?

TEACHING AIM
To lead adults to determine ways they will live so as to please God and win the respect of other people, especially people outside the church

LESSON ELEVEN
Live to Please God and Win Others' Respect

1 & 2 THESSALONIANS
Guidance for Healthy Church Life

BIBLE COMMENTS

Understanding the Context

In coming to the close of his letter, Paul laid out advice to the Thessalonians regarding how to conduct their lives with one another, towards outsiders, and ultimately with God. In the ancient world, this advice was known as *parenesis* and was used to encourage people to either start or stop some particular behavior. In order for a person or group to accept such advice, the messenger typically needed authority and credibility; for the Thessalonians, Paul had both.

Words of advice can be received as criticism and breed resentment. Paul's words, however, were dipped in encouragement. He had only the most optimistic outlook for the continued growth of the Thessalonians in faith. His was a confidence based on what he had already seen in their lives and a hope in what God would continue to do within them.

In presenting his advice, Paul called on the Thessalonians to remember previous instructions. The Thessalonians were not a blank slate but already had obtained through his and others' teachings, and even God's own implanted instruction, the knowledge needed to live worthy lives in the midst of a pagan culture.

To reinforce the parenesis, Paul also presented a series of sayings related to daily Christian conduct. Pithy sayings—such as "a stitch in time saves nine"—provide basic instructions about life. In like manner, the sayings written by Paul provided basic truths for beginners in the faith as they continued to take first steps in the Christian life.

Woven through all Paul's words of advice was the model of his own life in Christ. Just as the Thessalonians learned from Paul's actions, his hope was that others would see the actions of the Thessalonian believers and begin to imitate them by coming to faith in Jesus Christ. To model the Christian life for the people in Thessalonica was a large challenge for the believers in this city. By choosing to follow Christ, suspicion was raised about their activities and motives. Paul's advice provided a way to encourage the Thessalonians to keep faithful in their witness.

Interpreting the Scriptures

Living a Sanctified Life (4:1–8)

4:1–2. Paul's final words to the Thessalonians carried a sense of urgency as he asked them to live lives pleasing to God. The urgency was tempered by the positive affirmation that the Thessalonians were already living worthy lives. Paul was grateful they had learned in part some of their conduct from him and his coworkers. He encouraged them to excel in their new Christian lives with renewed and reinvigorated commitment.

4:3. The phrase "the will of God" is used to cover a multitude of purposes. Paul, however, provided a clear definition for the Thessalonians regarding the content of God's will: "sanctification." The root of this word means *to be holy*. In the ancient world, *to be holy* meant *being set apart*, not in pious isolation from others, but set apart to demonstrate one's special status and obligations.

Paul gave the Thessalonians a specific example of sanctification: abstaining from fornication. In Paul's day, Gentiles were stereotyped as having few if any positive sexual ethics. Paul, therefore, reinforced for his mainly Gentile Christian listeners the importance of high moral standards. "Fornication" meant *violating sexual boundaries*, such as by committing adultery.

4:4–5. These verses on sexual morality are notoriously difficult to translate and present two possibilities: (1) "that each one of you know how to control your own body [Greek, *skeuos*] in holiness and honor" (NRSV), or (2) "that each one of you know how to take a wife [*skeuos*] for himself in holiness and honor" (RSV). The word *skeuos* means "vessel" and was either a polite way to describe the male sex organ or, less likely, a way to describe a wife.

Paul condemned uncontrolled, misdirected, and excessive desires that resulted in treating another person as an object. In "lustful passion," a person only becomes an instrument for a self-satisfying goal. Paul clearly told the Thessalonians that such behavior had no room in a community striving for holiness and honor. While these verses are culturally specific in language, they still illustrate that one's actions define character. Conduct in sexual relationships or decisions related to food, clothing, or other objects will either honor God and demonstrate holiness or reveal a person who uses others and objects for personal ends.

4:6. Paul's advice to the Thessalonians continued by emphasizing that no one in the community of faith should exploit another. This exploitation could be sexual, following from the previous verse, or it could apply to any type of relationship. In community, bonds of trust are created, and Paul knew that, for the survival of the Thessalonians, mutual trust among believers was imperative. To take advantage of or wrong another destroys relationships and cripples community.

4:7–8. To highlight the seriousness of exploitation, Paul reminded the Thessalonians they were called into holiness. If they rejected Paul's advice about proper sexual conduct, they were rejecting not only Paul's authority but also God's desire for their lives, and by extension, the gift of the Holy Spirit. Such a dire warning would give the Thessalonians a significant pause when considering their ethical decisions.

Living a Simplified Life (4:9–12; 5:14–15)

4:9–10a. In these verses, Paul shifted from a focus on negative conduct to positive. Paul rejoiced in the Thessalonians' love for one another and that their love extended beyond the boundaries of Thessalonica to the believers in Macedonia. Paul described a love that overflows in liberality towards others.

The Thessalonians learned their lesson of love from the ultimate teacher: God. Paul coined a word to describe the learning experience: "taught by God." This lesson was an old one stretching back to the Old Testament command to love one's neighbor as oneself (Leviticus 19:18) and was also foundational for Jesus' preaching and teaching (Mark 12:29–32). Paul rejoiced that the Thessalonians had taken this lesson from God into their hearts and lived it out in the community.

4:10b–11. Having laid the foundation for living in love, Paul presented three rules for living an honorable life in the midst of Thessalonica. These rules described a lifestyle based on quietness, simplicity, and manual labor. Nothing flashy or extraordinary existed in these rules, and yet they represented a path to a stable community that could be admired by outsiders.

Living quietly and minding one's own affairs go together and imply avoiding excessive public engagement. Paul was giving practical advice to converts who had left paganism. No doubt the rejection of traditions and city deities caused tension in some quarters of Thessalonica. Paul's advice was not to withdraw from society. However, Paul also did not advise them to poke at a hornet's nest. The Thessalonians were to maintain a distinct and discreet lifestyle within the larger society.

Paul also urged the Thessalonians to work with their hands. The well-being of the community and the sharing of goods depended on the responsibility of each person. Paul wanted believers to practice communal self-sufficiency.

4:12. The reason for the simple and quiet lifestyle was to witness to outsiders. Paul did not call it evangelism, but practicing a distinctive Christian lifestyle is a mission model for attracting people. The lifestyle presents a vision of and an invitation to God's reign, especially in the midst of a broken world.

Another motive for Paul's advice was to avoid dependence on others. This independence could mean Paul did not want a person living like a parasite within the community. Paul hoped for a community of faith as a place for mutual sharing and interdependence. Paul may also have been instructing the community to earn respect from outsiders by not depending on their assistance. Dependence on outsiders reflected a community not looking after one another.

5:14. Paul gave four quick pieces of advice for believers. "To admonish the idlers" means to correct those who were either lazy or displayed disorderly behavior. Either way, these individuals did not have the mutual good of the community as their goal. The "faint-hearted" and the "weak" could represent the same group. Not only was one to encourage this group but also to find ways actively to assist those in crisis or tragedy. Paul concluded with one all-inclusive piece of advice for dealing with all types of situations within a community: "be patient with all of them."

5:15. "Repaying evil for evil" was a well-known saying for retaliation. Its foundation was rooted in the "eye for eye, tooth for tooth" (Exodus 21:24) approach and was an expected, maybe even required, response to injury. Paul, like Jesus before him (Matthew 5:38–39), dismantled this violent approach to life. He humanized relationships with others by advocating seeking always to do good to one another. What became radical and subversive in this approach was not only giving good to those within the community, but also "to all." Good was to be done even for those outsiders who antagonized and persecuted the community. Paul's dictum was simple and powerful: subvert evil with good.

Sayings to Live By (5:16–22)

5:16–18. In staccato fashion, Paul presented a series of sayings the Thessalonians were to stitch into the fabric of their lifestyle. Since Paul's world was mainly oral, these sayings were created to be remembered. The advice in these sayings is different from any previous advice because these sayings are grounded in one's responses to God: rejoicing, praying, and giving thanks.

The beginning advice, "rejoice always," is an acknowledgement that all good gifts come from God. It also contains the idea of joyful confidence in God, even when faced with distress or persecution. Since Paul had modeled an unceasing prayer life (1 Thess. 1:2), he urged the Thessalonians to follow his pattern of praying "without ceasing." Paul understood the Christian life as a wordless prayer offered up to God. The content of that prayer is found in Paul's next admonition, "give thanks in all circumstances." This type of prayer acknowledges God working in all situations, even the crises, to bring about wholeness and peace.

5:19–20. Paul presented two prohibitions for the Thessalonians: not quenching "the Spirit" and not despising the "words of prophets." Paul wanted the Thessalonians to avail themselves of guidance from the Spirit. Perhaps the Thessalonians were hesitant to follow the Spirit because to do so challenged cultural and societal norms. Paul also encouraged the Thessalonians to listen to the words of the prophets. Prophets in this context were not the Old Testament prophets, but either the local or itinerant prophets of Paul's day. The nearest equivalent today would be preachers. These prophets spoke words of comfort, exhortation, judgment, and insight. By listening to their words, the Thessalonians would extend their knowledge and growth in the faith, but, as the next bit of advice notes, they were to listen with a discerning ear.

5:21–22. Paul encouraged testing everything. Teachings, actions, and relationships that appear good on the surface may originate in corrupt motives and will eventually bloom into pollution and destruction. As Paul noted, evil has different forms. Many of them are beautiful and attractive. Only when a believer evaluates with both the mind and spirit can a trustworthy decision be made to avoid evil and embrace what is helpful, wise, correct, and truly good.

A Blessing for Sanctification (5:23–24)

5:23–24. By ending with a benediction, Paul captured his most heartfelt desire for the Thessalonians. He prayed for their holiness in all parts of their being (spirit, soul, and body). He concluded with an assurance that they would be holy and also prepared for the coming of Christ. Paul added that it was God who "will do this." After all the advice about conduct and actions, Paul ended by affirming once again grace over works righteousness. All that one is able to do and accomplish in living the Christian faith comes through the power and grace of God.

Focusing on the Meaning

In the ancient world, life was lived in public; little private space existed. Therefore, Paul realized his community would come under the scrutiny of outsiders. The conduct of this newly formed community of faith would be a window into how the reign of God was being lived out. The Thessalonians were a demonstration model of this reign of God. Paul wanted to remind the Thessalonians that they were always under the watchful eyes of their neighbors, who could either be engaged by the witness they saw or appalled by it.

Even though privacy is much more prevalent today, the situation of the Thessalonians is a reminder that the conduct within our churches, towards one another, and towards others, will be a witness either for or against Christ. Well-being and unity in the community of faith translates to witness for those outside the community. The popular phrase

WWJD, "what would Jesus do," could be adapted for Paul to the phrase *WWPW*, "what will people witness?"

The conduct Paul urged on the Thessalonians, and what he hoped outsiders witnessed, is summarized with two words: honor and holiness. These two characteristics represent the relationship Christians are called to exhibit between themselves and others and with God. Honor is the trait lived out in both internal community relationships and external relationships with society. Holiness is the covenantal relationship between God and Christians. Christians engaged in the process of practicing holiness have a new status and new obligations.

Paul also appealed to the Thessalonians to live a simple lifestyle and practice quiet faithfulness. This appeal is a challenge for many in our culture. Work has been depersonalized and made into a commodity. Paul, however, presented an alternative in the dignity of all honest and simple work. Paul's how-to-live in simplicity and quietness stands in sharp contrast to the peer pressure and cultural trends of today. His is a welcomed challenge to resist popular societal values and follow a distinctively Christian lifestyle.

TEACHING PLANS

Teaching Plan—Varied Learning Activities

Connect with Life

1. Divide into small groups of no more than six people each. To each group, hand out pieces of paper on which you have drawn a simple outline or stick figure of a person. Invite each group to sketch in the details of what would make an *ideal Christian*. For example, they might draw a large heart symbolizing a loving attitude, or a large purse or wallet symbolizing generosity. Encourage the group to have fun with the exercise. After a few minutes, ask each group to reveal their drawing and the details they've added. Alternatively,

you could draw the outline on the markerboard and lead the class in suggesting the details as you draw them, or allow people to draw in details themselves.

2. Stress that there is no such thing as an *ideal Christian*, but the Bible does give us some goals to strive toward. Some of these are written in 1 Thessalonians.

Guide Bible Study

3. Enlist someone to read 1 Thessalonians 4:1–8 while the class listens for Paul's instructions. Point out that the *Study Guide* uses the term "radar-directed people" to describe people who are concerned about the opinion of others. Suggest that the class imagine such a radar-directed person, first in the environment of the work place and then in the environment of your church. Ask, *In each environment, what cues or actions might this person detect, and how might he or she react?* If you like, form small groups, assigning half the groups to describe a radar-directed person in the workplace and the other half to describe a radar-directed person in your church environment. After a few minutes of discussion, call for reports.

4. Invite someone to read 1 Thessalonians 4:9–10. State: *Paul urged these people to love "more and more." Is it possible to control and grow how much we love other people? If so, how?*

    Refer to the section in the *Study Guide* subtitled "Love in the Church Family." Ask the class to think of someone in the church with whom they have difficulty getting along. Then ask them to think of the reasons for this situation, and their personal responsibility. Do they need to forgive someone or seek forgiveness? Do they need to confront the other person lovingly ? Allow members to respond privately. *Then ask, If we refuse to try to get along with people in the church, what difference does it make to the church itself? to ourselves?* Lead in silent prayer that God will reveal or clarify our opinions and attitudes, show us the proper pathway to resolving situations, and enable us to have the strength of character to do so.

5. Have someone read 1 Thessalonians 4:11–12 while the class listens for what would "win the respect of outsiders." Ask, *Assuming that Paul was directing these words to unacceptable attitudes and actions among the Thessalonians, what do you think the Thessalonians might have been doing? What might be some modern-day parallels Paul would warn against?*

   Point out this statement from the *Study Guide* in the second paragraph under the heading "Earn the Respect of Outsiders (4:11–12)": "Our goal is to please God. But when we do this the right way, we may win the respect of others as a bonus." Ask, *Can you think of some examples or scenarios about how this might work out? What about some example that are exceptions; that is, where people are pleasing God but not winning the respect of "outsiders"?*

6. Read 1 Thessalonians 5:14–22 slowly, pausing after each admonition. Ask, *Which one or two of these do you think is most difficult to do?* Receive reports. Then continue, *If we had a checklist for each of these, which ones would you be able to check, and which would you have to leave blank?* If you like, in advance prepare a checklist, make copies and distribute to each person in the class to use during this step. (A copy of such a checklist is available in "Teaching Resource Items" for this study at www.baptistwaypress.org.)

Encourage Application

7. Explain that sometimes people make wooden plaques or stitch samplers of favorite Bible verses or admonitions like the ones in this passage. Invite the class to review the entire passage and the various instructions and admonitions in it. Then they are to choose one or two that are personally meaningful, focusing on those that will lead them to live so as to please God and win the respect of other people, especially people outside the church. Next, ask how they would depict this admonition (assuming they had the time to do so!). Stitch a sampler? Paint a picture? Write a poem? Tool a wooden plaque? If you like, distribute paper and pencils or colored markers to each person so he or she can create a design. As time permits, ask as many people as possible to tell what they chose and how they would depict it.

Teaching Plan—Lecture and Questions

Connect with Life

1. In advance, make notes for yourself of several proverbs along the lines of "An apple a day keeps the doctor away" or "Early to bed and early to rise makes a man healthy wealthy and wise." Begin class by asking people to recall some proverbs like these that give instructions for how to live a good, healthy, successful life. Allow a few minutes for people to think of them and call them out; add your own as needed. Then say that today we will study Paul's message to the Thessalonians about living godly lives, including some short passages that have become proverbs.

Guide Bible Study

2. Enlist someone to read 1 Thessalonians 4:1–8 while the class listens for Paul's message. State that the main idea in this section is that Christians should live in a way that pleases God. Ask, *What are the key points you see in this section that characterize a life that pleases God?* Answers should include: avoiding sexual immorality, behaving properly toward other people, living pure and holy lives.

    Use questions such as these to lead a discussion:
    - Why do you think personal purity, especially with regard to sexual behavior, is so important to Paul and to God?
    - Is it possible to live a life that is pleasing to God when one is involved in sexual impurity?
    - What role does the Holy Spirit play in leading people to live lives pleasing to God?

    Caution: Deal carefully and lovingly with each person; remember and remind that God is the only one capable of judging people's hearts and actions.

3. Invite someone to read 1 Thessalonians 4:9–10 while the class listens for Paul's instructions about loving other people. Ask, *What do you think Paul meant when he said the Thessalonians had been "taught by God" to love one another? How do you think the Thessalonians*

demonstrated love to follow Christians throughout Macedonia, and how could they "do so more and more"?

4. Have someone read 1 Thessalonians 4:11–12. Call attention to the small article in the *Study Guide* titled "Heroes of the Faith." Ask the class to think of one or two people they know whom they consider a *hero of the faith* like one of these. Then, instruct them to turn to a partner and tell each other about their hero.

5. Read 1 Thessalonians 5:14–24. Note that the *Study Guide* emphasizes the verbs "warn"; "encourage"; "help"; and "be patient." Note, too, that Paul wanted Christian believers to do these for one another. Ask, *What are examples of opportunities we might have to do these things?* When might a Christian's loving concern for another person cross a line and become inappropriate or counterproductive?

Encourage Application

6. Refer to the small article, "Are You Going Further With Love?" Lead a time of prayer during which you pray about each of the points mentioned: Family; Church; Geographical Outreach; Racial Outreach; and Personal Attitude.

FOCAL TEXT

1 Thessalonians 4:13—5:11

BACKGROUND

1 Thessalonians 4:13—5:11;
2 Thessalonians 1:5—2:12

MAIN IDEA

The hope Christ offers through
his resurrection and promised
return provides guidance and
encouragement for life now
and assurance for eternity.

QUESTION TO EXPLORE

How does the hope Christ
offers affect your life in
both time and eternity?

TEACHING AIM

To lead adults to put into
their own words what the
hope Christ offers means
for their lives now and as
they consider eternity

LESSON TWELVE

*Hope for Time
and Eternity*

BIBLE COMMENTS

Understanding the Context

These verses contain references to the end of time, or the end of the age. The term frequently used to describe the study of *last things* is *eschatology*. Paul, like many other Jews, believed time could be divided into two ages: the present evil or fallen age and the blessed age to come. The present evil age was marked by struggles and persecution for the followers of God. These experiences intensified the more a believer lived out an honorable calling in a fallen world. The great hope was for the coming day of the Lord when all evil and corrupt elements within this world would be swept away. At that day, the reign of God would be fully experienced through a renewed world.

For Paul, this new age began with the resurrection of Jesus. First Thessalonians 4:12—5:11 illustrates that Paul's outlook on life was dominated by God raising Jesus from the dead. Jesus was the great sign, God's great *yes*, that the new age had broken into the old. However, the old age was still here. The Thessalonians knew this truth only too well because of persecution. Also, the old age weighed heavy upon the Thessalonians because some believers in their midst had experienced death.

Although the new age began at Jesus' resurrection, Paul reminded the Thessalonians that the final, perfect, and complete age would arrive only with Christ's return. The term frequently used to describe Christ's return is *parousia*, the Greek word meaning *return, advent,* or *coming*. The Thessalonians were confused over what this return of Christ meant, especially for those who had died since Paul's initial stay with them.

This lesson's text, especially 1 Thessalonians 4:16–17, presents some interpretative challenges. These verses are difficult to understand because Paul never again in any of his letters described what it means to "meet the Lord in the air." While individuals can get sidetracked on doctrinal issues in these verses, one should keep in mind the foundational truth Paul conveyed that, whether alive or dead, we can rest in the security of being present with Christ forever.

Interpreting the Scriptures

Reassurance for the Grieving (4:13–15)

4:13. During Paul's absence from the Thessalonians, some individuals within the community had "died" (literally, *fallen asleep*, a metaphor for death). Their deaths raised a deep concern within the church. For this reason, the Thessalonians turned for advice to their founding teacher. Their anxiety about the deceased was most likely conveyed through Timothy to Paul, and Paul chose to respond with this letter of reassurance.

The anxious grief of the Thessalonians probably occurred because they had not completely understood Paul's teaching while he was in their midst. Part of this misunderstanding was related to the resurrection of the dead, something Paul surely taught them, and the gathering of all to greet Christ at his return.

Paul did not condemn their grief at the loss of a loved one, but rather he challenged misplaced grief. One can grieve in hopelessness or one can grieve in hopefulness; Paul urged the latter. The pagan world had little hope for any life beyond death. A frequently abbreviated epitaph on pagan gravestones read "I was not, I am not, I care not." Such a sentiment illustrates that hope for pagans ended with the fresh dirt of a new grave.

4:14. Paul reminded the Thessalonians, even in their grief, that hope continued to exist because of Christ's resurrection. It was hope for all believers, both dead and living. For Paul, the resurrection of Jesus was a signal of the coming of the end. The idea of resurrection, of course, denoted different meanings to different groups. For the pagans, it was a ridiculous and unbelievable tale, and for the Jews it was an event only to occur at the end of the age. For Paul, resurrection was the power of God experienced each day through the witness of the Spirit.

4:15. Paul supported his reassurance of hope with the words "of the Lord." Perhaps Paul meant his words represented an unknown saying from Jesus or a paraphrased oral tradition from Jesus' teaching as found later in Mark 13 or Matthew 24. Paul may even have meant he received special revelation from God or passed on the recent revelation from a Christian prophet. Either way, Paul wanted to give weight to his reassurance for the Thessalonians.

Paul believed the dead in Christ would go ahead of those still alive when Christ returned. The dead were not disadvantaged but would participate fully in the triumphant return of Christ. Paul assumed Christ's return in his lifetime: "we who are alive, who are left until the coming of the Lord." Paul's words are a timely reminder against presuming to know the schedule of Christ's return.

Christ's Return Described (4:16–18)

4:16. Paul used both vivid and traditional language to describe the return of Christ. The vivid language captures the ear with its description of a cry of command, call of the archangel, and trumpet sound. The visual is also present in Paul's description of the descending Christ and gathering clouds in verse 17.

The language is also traditional because it draws on symbols from both Jewish and Roman backgrounds. In Jewish tradition, the trumpet frequently signaled critical moments in the life of Israel. The looming presence of the archangel often represented an end-of-the-age moment. In the midst of the audio and visual experience of the Lord's return, Paul reminded the Thessalonians again that participation came first for the resurrected ones—those who were "dead in Christ."

4:17. Only after the dead in Christ rose to meet the Lord would those alive be caught up to meet Christ. Here the Roman background helps explain Paul's image. In the ancient world people went out to greet approaching emperors or dignitaries. The people would then escort the honored person back to the city. Paul described both the dead and those who are alive as going up to meet Christ. This meeting was to escort him back to earth as he descends and brings God's kingdom to the world (4:16). In Paul's picture, the new age has fully come.

This verse should not be used to picture Christ coming down and then whisking only some people away. Rather, a straightforward reading illustrates meeting the Lord as he descends from heaven. The great promise in the prayer Jesus taught his disciples comes to reality in these verses: "Your kingdom come, your will be done, on earth as it is in heaven" (Matthew 6:10). Both the dead and living can rejoice on this kingdom day.

4:18. Paul ended his brief insight into Christ's return with the purpose for his words: encouragement. Paul provided pastoral care to his beloved children in Christ. He sought to give them words to repeat to one another during times of deep grief. One should remember Paul was not writing a systematic theology about the end of the age. Yet we often attempt to extract theological systems and schemes from Paul's words. His words were simply ones of care and comfort from a pastor to his hurting congregation.

The Coming Day of the Lord (5:1–5)

5:1. Paul, while still dealing with Christ's return, shifted his focus to describe in more detail the nature of the Lord's return. Paul reminded the Thessalonians he did not need to write further about the event because he had already taught the believers about what would happen. Paul, however, repeated at least one significant aspect of Christ's return to help the Thessalonians be prepared for this event.

5:2. Paul wrote that the day of the Lord would come like a "thief in the night." The "day of the Lord" was already a well-known phrase based on the Old Testament (Joel 2:31; Amos 5:18; Malachi 4:5). The day of the Lord was an eagerly anticipated moment when God's rule on earth would both bless and correct the world. This day would vindicate the persecuted and burdened and also purge evil from the world. The prophets, however, challenged individuals not to presume that the day of the Lord would always be in their favor. Right actions and the internal disposition of the heart determined how one encountered that day. For Paul, that day is characterized by suddenness. He used the arresting metaphor of a thief in the night.

5:3. With slogans like "there is peace and security," Paul captured with irony how unprepared people would be for Christ's return. Believing all was well, individuals would awaken in surprise. Paul expanded the image of suddenness with the experience of the swift onset of pain during child birth. This image provided the additional point that in Christ's return, just as in an anticipated birth, no escape exists; it will happen.

5:4–5. In the midst of words that might cause anxiety among his listeners, Paul commended them as children of light in contrast to children of darkness. Light and dark were two of the most powerful symbols in the ancient world. Light conveyed the sense of insight, life, and attentiveness to seeing. Paul felt assured that the Thessalonians would not be caught off guard, that is, in the dark when Christ returned. They had insight as children of light; they were insiders to the nature of the Lord's return.

Advice and Reassurance in Waiting (5:6–11)

5:6–7. In order to guarantee the Thessalonians were prepared for the day of the Lord, Paul gave them two direct commands: "keep awake and be sober." The first command called on the Thessalonians to cultivate the spirit of anticipation and expectation. The second command called on them to live out that anticipation with self control. Paul stressed to the Thessalonians that the Lord's return should energize ethical conduct for expectant Christians. The image of drunk and sober was a general metaphor meant to describe proper conduct in all aspects of Christian living, not only drinking.

5:8. Paul understood living an upright, honorable, and proper life could be a battle. For this reason, he employed military language: "breastplate" and "helmet." This battle, lived while awaiting Christ's return, engaged weapons of the Spirit, that is, Paul's well-known triad of faith, love, and hope. Just as Paul began his letter with these three virtues (1:3), he also ended his letter with them.

Paul qualified salvation by describing it as the "hope of salvation." For Paul, salvation was not an object to grasp and hold onto, but a future hope. Paul understood life as sanctification, or the process of becoming holy and living towards the goal of salvation. Paul never presumed on the grace of God in addressing the difficulty of the battles of life.

5:9–10. Although living the Christian faith was a battle, Paul ended on the positive note that God's hope and destiny for the Thessalonians was not destruction but salvation, that is, wholeness. They should not be discouraged because through Christ nothing would separate them from their relationship with God.

5:11. Just as Paul concluded by urging the Thessalonians to do pastoral care among themselves (4:18), he once again exhorted his listeners to mutual encouragement. Even though the Thessalonians had Paul's letter to read and pass around, Paul knew face-to-face encouragement within the community would steady and prepare them for any eventualities until the day of the Lord.

Focusing on the Meaning

As we reflect on Paul's final words in his First Letter to the Thessalonians, we do well to remember that he was not writing a *systematic* theology. Rather Paul wrote *pastoral* theology. As he learned about new situations and questions raised by the Thessalonians, he answered out of a deep sense of concern and love for his brothers and sisters. The undergirding foundation for Paul's pastoral theology to the Thessalonians was comfort. Paul wrote to encourage distressed, emotionally grieving, and uncertain believers.

In a world that seemed to be falling part, Paul strengthened the Thessalonians by reassuring them of a center that would hold. The center focused on the life, death, and resurrection of Jesus and also on the hope of his return. Marginal questions, such as the when and how of Christ's return, both excited and created anxiety for the Thessalonians, but Paul never drifted from his focus on Christ. This focus gave direction and clarity for living out the faith.

Paul's words can encourage contemporary believers who experience times of anxiety in life. Often those times of anxiety come at moments of crisis. Words of encouragement come not only from Paul but also from respected teachers or leaders, and one another. Mutual encouragement within one's community can guide one through difficult times.

Perhaps one of the greatest assurances found in these verses is the ever-present relationship of God with us in Christ. Paul reassured the Thessalonians that the dead would always be with God, because they died "in Christ." To live and to die in Christ meant being enveloped in the cloak of Christ. Nothing, not even death, can separate the relationship between God and God's new creation as found in believers. When faced with the loss of a loved one or our own impending death, this assurance becomes more than ink on a page or a pious platitude. This assurance is the balm of encouragement for sinking souls.

TEACHING PLANS

Teaching Plan—Varied Learning Activities

Connect with Life

1. Begin by suggesting that people have always had questions about how God works and about God's timing. Point out that our passage today deals with questions the Thessalonians had about their loved ones who had died and about Christ's return. Note that we will see that their questions are similar to ours and that the answers they received from Paul are helpful to us.

Guide Bible Study

2. Enlist someone to read 1 Thessalonians 4:13–18 while the class listens for Paul's message. Explain that Paul was writing to people who were worried about loved ones who had already died. Ask, *Why do you think Paul used the term "fall asleep"?* Use information in the *Study Guide* and "Bible Comments" in this *Teaching Guide* to explain 4:13–18. Refer to verse 18, and ask why the previous verses would have been encouraging.

3. Invite someone to read 1 Thessalonians 5:1–3. Note that Paul used two images here to convey the suddenness of the Second Coming: a thief in the night; and the beginning of labor pains for a pregnant woman. Ask, *What are some other examples of events that may occur with little or no warning?* Examples could include tornadoes, earthquakes, car wrecks, and so on. If you like, jot the examples on the markerboard. Also ask, *Can you think of examples of good*

things that happen with little or no warning? Continue, *Why do you think Paul emphasized that the Day of the Lord, or the Second Coming of Christ, would occur with no warning?*

4. Refer to the list of unexpected occurrences and say, *It is always a good idea to be prepared for events like these. What are some items you would put into an emergency preparedness kit?* Allow the class to name items such as candles, water, first aid kit, etc.

   Have someone read 1 Thessalonians 5:4–11. State that Paul had some instructions to the Thessalonians about being prepared as they awaited the unexpected Day of the Lord. Ask, *What do you see in this passage that you could include in a spiritual emergency preparedness kit?* Guide the class to include "alert . . . self-controlled . . . faith and love as a breastplate . . . the hope of salvation as a helmet." Add any other thoughts they suggest. Use information in the *Study Guide* and "Bible Comments" in this *Teaching Guide* to explain 5:4–11.

Encourage Application

5. Divide into small groups (no more than six people in each). Read the following case study to the class, or prepare copies for each group. (A copy is available in "Teaching Resource Items" for this study at www.baptistwaypress.org.) Instruct the groups to answer the questions. Call for reports after a few minutes of work time.

   Shawn, a young adult friend, has recently accepted Christ as Lord and Savior. Shawn's cousin in another state died recently. Although they were not close, Shawn is troubled about what has happened to this cousin and unsure about what will happen when he himself dies.

   - Using this lesson's Scripture passage, what words of comfort could you offer Shawn about the cousin's death?
   - What would you say if the cousin were not a Christian believer?
   - What would you advise Shawn to do in preparation for the Second Coming or his own death?
   - What does the hope Christ offers mean for your life now and as you consider eternity?

Close with prayer that each person may find comfort and challenge in living life as we wait for Christ's return.

Teaching Plan—Lecture and Questions

Connect with Life

1. Lead the class to recall a time when they lost something of value. After allowing the group a moment to think, follow up with these questions:
   - Did the object's value, monetary or sentimental, make a difference in how diligently you searched for the item?
   - Did it make a difference if you were pretty sure you would find it (for example, if you were positive it was somewhere in your home)?
   - How did you feel when you lost the item and then when you found it or gave up on finding it?

   Allow people to answer the questions for themselves, or lead a discussion among the class.

2. State that when we lose items, we have varying emotions depending on how deeply we value the item and how assured we are that the item will turn up. We may also have varying emotions when we lose someone to death, depending on the nature of our relationship and our understanding of what happens to people after they die. Point out that this study passage includes Paul's words of reassurance to his friends in Thessalonica regarding their worries about people who died.

Guide Bible Study

3. Ask the class to read 1 Thessalonians 4:13–18 silently. Lead a discussion with questions such as the following:
   - What do people, Christians as well as non-believers, like to believe about what happens after death?
   - Does knowing that a believer will be "with the Lord"

through eternity help when we contemplate our death or the death of someone we care about? If so, how?
- For whom does 1 Thessalonians 4:13–18 hold out hope?

4. Enlist someone to read 1 Thessalonians 5:1–3. Lead a discussion using the following questions:
   - Why have people through the ages tried to predict when the Second Coming will occur?
   - Can you think of some Bible verses indicating that God is the only one who knows when the Second Coming will occur? (Mark 13:32; see also Matthew 24:38–44; Acts 1:7) Why do you think God does not reveal the time?
   - What do you think Paul had in mind with the reference to people saying "Peace and safety" in 5:3?

5. Invite someone to read 1 Thessalonians 5:4–11. On the markerboard, make two columns. Label one column "Thessalonian Believers" and the second column "Others." Invite the class to review 1 Thessalonians 4:1; 5:4–9. List in the appropriate column the contrasts Paul cited between the Thessalonian believers and others. Ask, *Who would these "others" be for the Thessalonians? Do we personally know "others" like these?*

6. Note that Paul used the term "asleep" several times in our focal passage, 1 Thessalonians 4:13–18; 5:1–11. Ask:
   - Where did Paul use "asleep" to mean people who have died? (4:13–14)
   - Where did he use it to mean people who are sleeping? (5:7)
   - Where did he use it to indicate spiritual dullness? (5:6)
   - What do you think he meant by "asleep" in 1 Thessalonians 5:10? (Note: The Greek term in 4:13–14 is generally considered a euphemism for death. The alternate term, used in 5:6,7,10, can mean either *sleep* or *death*.)

Encourage Application

7. Use questions 1–5 in the *Study Guide* to lead a discussion.

8. Distribute pen and paper to each person. Invite each one to write in his or her own words what hope and reassurance this passage provides about future life in Christ—for life now and for eternity. Encourage people to keep this note in their Bibles. Invite sharing of this note, but make it easy for people not to do so.

You may have people in your class who have not come to believe in Christ as Savior or who are shaky in their belief. Announce that you are available to talk with them and help them find answers to their questions.

FOCAL TEXT
2 Thessalonians 3:1–16

BACKGROUND
2 Thessalonians 3

MAIN IDEA
Being a thriving church in a tough situation calls for relying on God's strength and the support of one's fellow believers; being faithful in one's daily life, including at work; and following Christian teachings.

QUESTION TO EXPLORE
What does being a thriving church in a tough situation require?

TEACHING AIM
To lead adults to develop a plan for becoming a thriving church in a tough situation, even in a truly pagan culture

LESSON THIRTEEN

Being a Thriving Church in a Tough Situation

BIBLE COMMENTS

Understanding the Context

In many ways, 2 Thessalonians has points of continuity with 1 Thessalonians but also points of disconnection. Both letters indicate persecution was a reality and that believers displayed endurance in the face of it. Also the theme of the day of the Lord occurs in both, although a different emphasis is placed on the nature of its arrival. In 1 Thessalonians, it arrived like a "thief in the night" (1 Thessalonians 5:2). In 2 Thessalonians, many signs would accompany its arrival; no one could miss it. Another point of commonality is the idleness of some believers. Especially in 2 Thessalonians 3:6–12, Paul reinforced and expanded teachings he had mentioned but not developed in 1 Thessalonians.

A significant aspect for understanding the focal verses is the social context of the believers to whom Paul wrote. Many of the congregations of Paul's day were made up of two different groups: the elites who had resources; and the non-elites who had little and eked out a bare existence. The relationship that often formed between these two groups was a patron-client relationship. In the context of Thessalonica, perhaps some of the clients were presuming on the good will, grace, and love of a few of the wealthy patrons. Charity and giving were, and are, a foundation for Christian practice; yet abuse could happen on either side. Elites could be stingy, and non-elites could be presumptuous.

As was typical in 1 Thessalonians, Paul set up a contrast between his behavior and what was being practiced at Thessalonica in 2 Thessalonians. The use of modeling and personal example continued to be a primary method for Paul's instruction to believers. Paul, however, did not use his personal actions alone as an example to follow; he also pointed to the conduct of his colleagues. The focus on Paul and his colleagues is a reminder that he lived and thought in a communal dimension. To read 2 Thessalonians 3:1–16 is to hear Paul's concern for communal relationships and dynamics. The individualism of modern interpreters needs to be tempered as they attempt to hear Paul in his world and on his own terms.

Interpreting the Scriptures

Prayerful Requests (3:1–5)

3:1. While Paul frequently prayed on behalf of the Thessalonians (1 Thess. 1:2; 3:10, 2 Thess. 1:11), he also relished prayers for himself and his coworkers (1 Thess. 5:25). The success of Paul's mission work included the intercessory prayers offered up in local congregations. The specific object of Paul's request was that the gospel of Christ might "spread" (literally, *run*) across the Mediterranean world. This image is a vivid one of God's word sprinting with Spirit-fed energy from city to city. Paul prayed for the increasing glory of the good news as it spread and as individuals heard and accepted it.

3:2. Paul added, almost as an afterthought, a brief personal request for the well-being of himself and his coworkers. He asked for relief from people he called "wicked" and "evil." These labels appear stark and harsh, and the identity of these individuals is not clear. However, from what can be gathered in 1 and 2 Thessalonians and later letters, Paul often encountered opposition to the message he brought (see 1 Thess. 2:14–16 and 2 Corinthians 11:23–29). One person's good news becomes a threat to another person's way of life. Those threatened individuals could and did direct verbal and physical abuse towards Paul and his colleagues.

3:3. Although Paul began by asking for prayers, he could not restrain himself from praying for the Thessalonians. He reassured them that the faithful Lord would strengthen and guard them from the evil one. Just as Paul believed in the Spirit of the Lord as a faithful and sustaining force for believers, he also understood the evil one as a force of opposition and harassment. He looked beneath the surface and behind the curtain for the cause of obstacles in the lives of the Thessalonians. Paul's prayer reminds the reader of the Lord's Prayer and the petition: "deliver us from evil (*the evil one*)" (Matthew 6:13b).

3:4. Paul praised the Thessalonians for how they followed his earlier instructions. A certain level of irony, however, exists with this affirmation. While he was confident in the Lord about their response to his previous words, the next few verses (2 Thess. 3:6–12) illustrate that not everyone in the community practiced the Christian lifestyle Paul envisioned. Paul walked a fine line between correcting behavior and not discouraging new believers.

3:5. In his closing prayer, Paul asked for two grants of blessing for the hearts of the Thessalonians: the love of God and the steadfastness of Christ. Paul focused on these two actions being directed to the hearts of believers. In the ancient world, the heart was not the place of emotion but of the will. The heart represented the inner disposition of a person that ultimately determined one's actions.

In preparation for Paul's coming demands, he used the phrase the "love of God." This phrase meant the Thessalonians should consider how God loved them, and this model of God's action would encourage their own right behaviors. Likewise the prayer for hearts directed to the "steadfastness of Christ" meant that Christ's obedience and endurance was a pattern for the Thessalonians to follow as they contemplated how to live their lives with one another and in the larger culture.

The Christian Work Ethic (3:6–12)

3:6. Paul issued to the believers a succinct command to avoid any idle believers. Evidently this group disregarded Paul's earlier instructions about how to labor within the new community of faith. Paul's sharp rebuke raises several questions. Was this group small or large? Why had they neglected Paul's instruction? What was the cause of their idleness? What was the situation? While many of these questions cannot be answered, nevertheless Paul was passionate for the Thessalonians to exclude any relationships with idlers. He stamped his command with the authority of "our Lord Jesus Christ."

3:7. Paul reminded the Thessalonians they should have followed the example set by himself and his coworkers; they "were not idle." Paul's slogan was "imitate us." Far from an egotistical declaration, Paul's command reveals the truth that actions and personal example are the most persuasive methods for conveying truth. How one walks speaks much louder than how one talks. Paul set a high ethical bar for the Thessalonians in relationship to each person's work responsibility within the community.

3:8–9. Writing as if the Thessalonians had instructional amnesia, Paul gave several proofs for his model of energetic self-sufficiency. He said that he ate only when he gave appropriate compensation for his food. He called the Thessalonians to remember his persistent work "day and night" in their midst. In a not too subtle reminder, he pointed out that all his work he did willingly, even though he had the right as an apostle for the community to maintain him (1 Corinthians 9:4–19). Paul revealed a helpful truth at this point—to model love in action, one foregoes rights and privileges.

Paul's goal was self-sufficiency to avoid burdening and being dependent on the Thessalonians. This goal was achieved in no small measure by extreme sacrifice on Paul's behalf since he accomplished it through "toil and labor." Both terms denote extreme effort. He had hoped his effort would furnish for them both the pattern and motive for lives of self-sufficiency.

3:10. Paul repeated a proverb previously given to the Thessalonians: "Anyone unwilling to work should not eat." Some individuals consciously choose *not to work*, that is, they were "unwilling." Importantly, Paul did not condemn those *unable to work*. Charity continued to be a graceful gift to those in need. In prodding the Thessalonians out of their lethargic ways, Paul sought to teach them the Christian way of simplicity and honor in work.

3:11. Paul diagnosed one symptom of idleness: being a busybody. In this description, Paul made a play on Greek words captured by some English translations: "they are not busy, they are busybodies" (NIV). The idea behind "busybodies" is *meddling in the affairs of others*. A contemporary saying is, *Sticking one's nose in someone else's business*. Such meddling disrupts and strains relationships.

3:12. Paul presented directly to the idle the simple remedy for idleness: work quietly and earn one's own living. Paul had already reminded the Thessalonians of this approach to life in his earlier letter (1 Thess. 4:11–12). This type of lifestyle would bring stability to the community and also reap honor from outsiders who witnessed the mutual sharing and work of the Thessalonians. Paul's command to the idlers was a direct and forceful call for their repentance from their current lifestyle.

Final Words of Instruction (3:13–16)

3:13. Paul had addressed the idlers, but now he turned his attention to all believers in Thessalonica. Perhaps he feared that some believers might take his words to an extreme and withhold charity and compassion from those in need. He urged believers to do what was right. Whether in physical or spiritual exhaustion, Paul encouraged the Thessalonians to find strength in extending kindness to others.

3:14. Paul's instruction *to shame* any who did not heed his command may sound harsh to modern ears. Of course, shame only for the sake of humiliating another is always wrong. In the ancient world, however, shame could have a redemptive purpose. Paul hoped the excommunication of idlers would cause them to rethink their conduct and bring them back into fellowship. By being in exile, perhaps the idlers would realize the significance of being in community and in fellowship with others.

3:15. Paul warned the community that this exclusion from the community for discipline could easily slip into treating fellow believers as enemies. Paul urged his listeners to still acknowledge the idlers as believers, although as ones in need of correction. Paul wanted the Thessalonians to reflect on their attitude and motivation even towards disruptive and difficult members. He did not want a bad situation to become a tragic situation.

3:16. Perhaps in concern for the potential conflict generated by his words, Paul's last wish for the Thessalonians was for "peace" (*shalom*). Paul reminded them that Christ was "the Lord of peace" whose reign and subjects should be governed by peace. This peace, given by Christ, was more than just the absence of conflict but entailed the total well-being and wholeness of both the community and the individual. Paul prayed that this peace was inclusive of "all times in all ways."

Focusing on the Meaning

The gospel of Jesus Christ, while good news for the whole world, was not, and is not, always received as good news by everyone. The rejection of Paul's message often was accompanied by inhospitality, unkindness, and even more painful responses. In the face of such experiences, what was an apostle or a local believer to do? First—pray. As Paul knew, the success of any mission for God is dependent upon it being a mission *for God*. Prayer was the way to confirm the divine origin of the mission and to be receptive to the energy and passion of God's Spirit within it. Prayer also is one way believers can unite during tough situations.

Paul illustrated that these tough situations come both from outside (persecution) and inside (internal church conflict). Perhaps the most challenging situations are those that occur within a church. To live closely in community is to see one another at our best—and at our worst. How one handles conflict sets the stage frequently for the success or failure of ministry and mission to those outside the church. For this reason, Paul was adamant about resolving the difficult situation of idleness within the church at Thessalonica.

Paul resolved tough situations with practicality, common sense, and reliance on God's Spirit. The conflict at Thessalonica could be resolved by simply working quietly and earning one's own living. Paul drew on the deep wisdom tradition of putting one's hand to the task with all of a person's ability (Ecclesiastes 9:10). His words also remind us about measuring our achievements on a different standard: earn and live simply on what is enough. His words also challenge us to recognize in the work of others the goodness of what their hands have created.

What could be overlooked in these verses is the depth of theological insight Paul offered as he gave practical advice. While he gave instructions for a down-to-earth and simple pattern for living out one's faith, he also illustrated that one's faith is tested and proven in the everyday arenas of life. The most difficult tests and tough situations do not always wave bold headlines of crises. Rather, our faith is watered and nurtured in tough common everyday experiences. In such experiences, like Paul, we live out our faith with other believers and before non-believers.

TEACHING PLANS

Teaching Plan—Varied Learning Activities

Connect with Life

1. Divide into groups of three to five by counting off (so all the *ones* are in group one, etc.). The purpose is to mix people with folks they might not know as well as they know others. Give each group a paper bag with an assortment of items such as these: a bar of soap; five toothpicks; two rubber bands; three paper clips; two pieces of construction paper; some cotton balls; one piece of chewing gum. Select materials for the bag depending on what is handy. Tell each group they have five minutes to construct a church with a steeple using the materials in the bag. Start keeping time. Have *show and tell* at the end of five minutes.

   After *show and tell*, ask, *How was your experience of working as a group to do this project? What went well? What were some obstacles?* Allow time for responses, focusing on the personal interactions within the group rather than the work product.

   Say that churches—both now and in the time of Paul and the Thessalonians—are always challenged to work together for a common purpose. State: *Let's see what advice Paul gave to his friends in Thessalonica.*

Guide Bible Study

2. Call for someone to read 2 Thessalonians 3:1–5. Explain that this passage underscores how churches are to rely on prayer for God's direction, protection, and strength. Find out whether your church has a specific prayer ministry or committee, and invite a representative to come and talk about this group—how they enlist people to help, how they obtain prayer requests, how they organize themselves, what kind of feedback they give and receive, etc. If your church does not have a prayer ministry, lead the group to brainstorm how they as a group could help initiate such a ministry.

3. Invite someone to read 2 Thessalonians 3:6–16. Lead a discussion using questions such as these:
   - What problems did Paul address in this passage?
   - Some people might have quit working because they expected Jesus would return almost immediately. Why was their ceasing to work not acceptable to Paul?
   - What kinds of work do you think Paul had in mind?
   - Not every person who is willing to work is able to do so: some are disabled or unemployed. What are some ways they still can make a vital contribution to the work of a church? Refer to the comments about Operation Andrew in the introduction to the lesson in the *Study Guide*.

4. Point out that Paul exhorted the Thessalonians to persevere in "doing what is right" (3:13). Read the following case study and ask the class to respond.

   Terry has been praying for Happy Hills Church every day since joining a few years ago. Terry prays that the church might increase the number of baptisms, the pledges and donations to the budget, and weekly attendance at worship and Sunday School. Even so, there has been no noticeable increase in any of these measures. Terry has expressed discouragement to you. How might you respond?

Encourage Application

5. Divide the class into three groups and assign each group to imagine and consider the circumstances and viewpoint of one of the following people groups in your community: homeless people; young adults; and unchurched well-to-do people. Each small group should answer the following questions:

   (1) What are at least three important actions Paul wanted the church at Thessalonica to take according to 2 Thessalonians 3:1–16?

   (2) How would this people group evaluate your church in terms of these actions?

   (3) What are some things your church could begin to do to incorporate these actions into its life?

(A copy of these instructions is available in "Teaching Resource Items" for this study at www.baptistwaypress.org.)

Conclude with prayer that your church will be a thriving church in its own unique situation.

Teaching Plan—Lecture and Questions

Connect with Life

1. On the markerboard, make two columns labeled "Positive" and "Negative." Ask the class to recall recent news stories about churches and to note for each whether the story was positive or negative. Make a mark in the applicable column. After a few minutes of recollection, analyze which column has more marks, that is, whether the majority of the stories depicting actions of churches are positive or negative.

   State: *We must remember that the news naturally tends to pick up on a negative story more readily than a positive story. However, what may the negative marks suggest about how churches today may be perceived by the world around them?* After responses, say, *In today's passage, we will look at some principles churches should strive toward in order to thrive in today's "pagan" society.*

Guide Bible Study

2. Enlist someone to read 2 Thessalonians 3:1–5 while the class listens for the prayer concerns mentioned. State: *This passage is full of prayer concerns. What issues did Paul ask the Thessalonians to pray for?* (See 3:1–2.) *What issues was Paul praying about for them?* (See 3:5; consider also 3:3–4.)

   State that in verses 3–5, Paul expressed great confidence in how God would protect and strengthen the Thessalonians. Ask, *How does this confidence—which presumably applies to present-day believers as well—influence your thoughts and prayers?*

3. Invite someone to read 2 Thessalonians 3:6–16. Using the information in the *Study Guide* section "Thriving Churches Work," and

"Bible Comments" in this *Teaching Guide*, explain more fully about the problem Paul was addressing in the church of Thessalonica. Ask, *Why do you think Paul was so insistent that he and his associates did not depend on the Thessalonians for their support?*

4. Lead the group to focus on the thoughts in this passage about how the Thessalonians' Christian faith was to relate to their work. Refer to and explain verses 6–12 especially, using information in "Bible Comments" in this *Teaching Guide*. Ask, *How does your work influence the life you lead for the Lord? How does your Christian life influence your work?*

5. Point out that according to this passage, a church should rely on mutual prayer, should have members who are engaged in their occupations as well as in the work of the church, and should live at peace rather than being "mere busybodies" (3:11). Ask, *What are some things these instructions suggest to you about life in our church?*

   Review the *Study Guide* section "Thriving Churches Work," especially the last paragraph. Ask, *What are some things our church is doing in this area? What can we do better?*

6. Refer to and read or summarize the small article, "Church Discipline," in the *Study Guide*. Lead a discussion with questions such as these:
   • Have you known a church that exercised discipline over its members? What was the result?
   • What is the difference between imposing discipline and making disciples?
   • Should the church be more rigorous in imposing discipline on wayward members?
   • Should the church be more rigorous in the way it makes disciples of new members?
   • Which is more important? Making disciples or imposing discipline?

Encourage Application

7. Ask, *In what ways was the Thessalonian church facing a tough situation?* (Answers could include its small size, mixed demographics, lack of tradition to follow, hostility from some Jews and Gentiles, etc.)

   Then ask, *In what ways does our church face tough situations?* (Answers may be both similar and different.)

   State: *This passage and our lesson show that a church can thrive in a tough situation if it takes action.* Refer to the Main Idea in the *Study Guide.* Follow by asking, *Where is our church strong, and where do we need improvement on each of these?* Close with prayer for your church.

How to Order More Bible Study Materials

It's easy! Just fill in the following information. For additional Bible study materials, see www.baptistwaypress.org or get a complete order form of available materials by calling 1-866-249-1799 or e-mailing baptistway@bgct.org.

Title of item	Price	Quantity	Cost

This Issue:

Galatians and 1&2 Thessalonians—Study Guide (BWP001080)	$3.55	_____	_____
Galatians and 1&2 Thessalonians—Large Print Study Guide (BWP001081)	$3.95	_____	_____
Galatians and 1&2 Thessalonians—Teaching Guide (BWP001082)	$3.95	_____	_____

Additional Issues Available:

Growing Together in Christ—Study Guide (BWP001036)	$3.25	_____	_____
Growing Together in Christ—Large Print Study Guide (BWP001037)	$3.55	_____	_____
Growing Together in Christ—Teaching Guide (BWP001038)	$3.75	_____	_____
Participating in God's Mission—Study Guide (BWP001077)	$3.55	_____	_____
Participating in God's Mission—Large Print Study Guide (BWP001078)	$3.95	_____	_____
Participating in God's Mission—Teaching Guide (BWP001079)	$3.95	_____	_____
Genesis 12—50: Family Matters—Study Guide (BWP000034)	$1.95	_____	_____
Genesis 12—50: Family Matters—Teaching Guide (BWP000035)	$2.45	_____	_____
Leviticus, Numbers, Deuteronomy—Study Guide (BWP000053)	$2.35	_____	_____
Leviticus, Numbers, Deuteronomy—Large Print Study Guide (BWP000052)	$2.35	_____	_____
Leviticus, Numbers, Deuteronomy—Teaching Guide (BWP000054)	$2.95	_____	_____
Joshua, Judges—Study Guide (BWP000047)	$2.35	_____	_____
Joshua, Judges—Large Print Study Guide (BWP000046)	$2.35	_____	_____
Joshua, Judges—Teaching Guide (BWP000048)	$2.95	_____	_____
1 and 2 Samuel—Study Guide (BWP000002)	$2.35	_____	_____
1 and 2 Samuel—Large Print Study Guide (BWP000001)	$2.35	_____	_____
1 and 2 Samuel—Teaching Guide (BWP000003)	$2.95	_____	_____
1 and 2 Kings: Leaders and Followers—Study Guide (BWP001025)	$2.95	_____	_____
1 and 2 Kings: Leaders and Followers Large Print Study Guide (BWP001026)	$3.15	_____	_____
1 and 2 Kings: Leaders and Followers Teaching Guide (BWP001027)	$3.45	_____	_____
Ezra, Haggai, Zechariah, Nehemiah, Malachi—Study Guide (BWP001071)	$3.25	_____	_____
Ezra, Haggai, Zechariah, Nehemiah, Malachi—Large Print Study Guide (BWP001072)	$3.55	_____	_____
Ezra, Haggai, Zechariah, Nehemiah, Malachi—Teaching Guide (BWP001073)	$3.75	_____	_____
Job, Ecclesiastes, Habakkuk, Lamentations—Study Guide (BWP001016)	$2.75	_____	_____
Job, Ecclesiastes, Habakkuk, Lamentations—Large Print Study Guide (BWP001017)	$2.85	_____	_____
Job, Ecclesiastes, Habakkuk, Lamentations—Teaching Guide (BWP001018)	$3.25	_____	_____
Psalms and Proverbs—Study Guide (BWP001000)	$2.75	_____	_____
Psalms and Proverbs—Large Print Study Guide (BWP001001)	$2.85	_____	_____
Psalms and Proverbs—Teaching Guide (BWP001002)	$3.25	_____	_____
Matthew: Hope in the Resurrected Christ—Study Guide (BWP001066)	$3.25	_____	_____
Matthew: Hope in the Resurrected Christ—Large Print Study Guide (BWP001067)	$3.55	_____	_____
Matthew: Hope in the Resurrected Christ—Teaching Guide (BWP001068)	$3.75	_____	_____
Mark: Jesus' Works and Words—Study Guide (BWP001022)	$2.95	_____	_____
Mark: Jesus' Works and Words—Large Print Study Guide (BWP001023)	$3.15	_____	_____
Mark:Jesus' Works and Words—Teaching Guide (BWP001024)	$3.45	_____	_____
Jesus in the Gospel of Mark—Study Guide (BWP000066)	$1.95	_____	_____
Jesus in the Gospel of Mark—Large Print Study Guide (BWP000065)	$1.95	_____	_____
Jesus in the Gospel of Mark—Teaching Guide (BWP000067)	$2.45	_____	_____
Luke: Journeying to the Cross—Study Guide (BWP000057)	$2.35	_____	_____
Luke: Journeying to the Cross—Large Print Study Guide (BWP000056)	$2.35	_____	_____
Luke: Journeying to the Cross—Teaching Guide (BWP000058)	$2.95	_____	_____
The Gospel of John: The Word Became Flesh—Study Guide (BWP001008)	$2.75	_____	_____
The Gospel of John: The Word Became Flesh—Large Print Study Guide (BWP001009)	$2.85	_____	_____
The Gospel of John: The Word Became Flesh—Teaching Guide (BWP001010)	$3.25	_____	_____
Acts: Toward Being a Missional Church—Study Guide (BWP001013)	$2.75	_____	_____
Acts: Toward Being a Missional Church—Large Print Study Guide (BWP001014)	$2.85	_____	_____
Acts: Toward Being a Missional Church—Teaching Guide (BWP001015)	$3.25	_____	_____
Romans: What God Is Up To—Study Guide (BWP001019)	$2.95	_____	_____
Romans: What God Is Up To—Large Print Study Guide (BWP001020)	$3.15	_____	_____
Romans: What God Is Up To—Teaching Guide (BWP001021)	$3.45	_____	_____
Ephesians, Philippians, Colossians—Study Guide (BWP001060)	$3.25	_____	_____
Ephesians, Philippians, Colossians—Large Print Study Guide (BWP001061)	$3.55	_____	_____
Ephesians, Philippians, Colossians—Teaching Guide (BWP001062)	$3.75	_____	_____

1, 2 Timothy, Titus, Philemon—Study Guide (BWP000092)	$2.75	_____	_____
1, 2 Timothy, Titus, Philemon—Large Print Study Guide (BWP000091)	$2.85	_____	_____
1, 2 Timothy, Titus, Philemon—Teaching Guide (BWP000093)	$3.25	_____	_____
Revelation—Study Guide (BWP000084)	$2.35	_____	_____
Revelation—Large Print Study Guide (BWP000083)	$2.35	_____	_____
Revelation—Teaching Guide (BWP000085)	$2.95	_____	_____

Coming for use beginning December 2009

(a special 18-session study from Christmas to Easter: the price of the study reflects the additional number of lessons)

The Gospel of Luke—Study Guide (BWP001085)	$4.90	_____	_____
The Gospel of Luke—Large Print Study Guide (BWP001086)	$5.45	_____	_____
The Gospel of Luke—Teaching Guide (BWP001087)	$5.45	_____	_____

Cost
of items (Order value)   _____

Shipping charges
(see chart*)   _____

TOTAL   _____

Standard (UPS/Mail) Shipping Charges*

Order Value	Shipping charge**	Order Value	Shipping charge**
$.01—$9.99	$6.50	$160.00—$199.99	$22.00
$10.00—$19.99	$8.00	$200.00—$249.99	$26.00
$20.00—$39.99	$9.00	$250.00—$299.99	$28.00
$40.00—$59.99	$10.00	$300.00—$349.99	$32.00
$60.00—$79.99	$11.00	$350.00—$399.99	$40.00
$80.00—$99.99	$12.00	$400.00—$499.99	$48.00
$100.00—$129.99	$14.00	$500.00—$599.99	$58.00
$130.00—$159.99	$18.00	$600.00—$799.99	$70.00**

*Plus, applicable taxes for individuals and other taxable entities (not churches) within Texas will be added. Please call 1-866-249-1799 if the exact amount is needed prior to ordering.

**For order values $800.00 and above, please call 1-866-249-1799 or check www.baptistwaypress.org

Please allow three weeks for standard delivery. For express shipping service: Call 1-866-249-1799 for information on additional charges.

YOUR NAME _____   PHONE _____

YOUR CHURCH _____   DATE ORDERED _____

SHIPPING ADDRESS _____

CITY _____   STATE _____   ZIP CODE _____

E-MAIL _____

MAIL this form with your check for the total amount to
BAPTISTWAY PRESS, Baptist General Convention of Texas,
333 North Washington, Dallas, TX 75246-1798
(Make checks to "Baptist Executive Board.")

OR, **FAX** your order anytime to: 214-828-5376, and we will bill you.

OR, **CALL** your order toll-free: 1-866-249-1799
(M-Th 8:30 a.m.-6:00 p.m.; Fri 8:30 a.m.-5:00 p.m. central time),
and we will bill you.

OR, **E-MAIL** your order to our internet e-mail address:
baptistway@bgct.org, and we will bill you.

OR, **ORDER ONLINE** at www.baptistwaypress.org.

We look forward to receiving your order! Thank you!